MW00813609

Values-based Service for Sustainable Business

The role of values in developing and managing service companies has been under-researched in the existing literature – until now. This book analyzes a large organization (IKEA) as a basis for values-based service for sustainable business.

The authors provide an overview of the history of IKEA and the social and environmental perspectives that have acted as driving forces for creating economic value. They go on to develop values-based service thinking within the areas of service experience, service brand, and service leadership. The book concludes by comparing IKEA with other values-based service companies (such as Starbucks, H&M, and Body Shop); from these reflections, the book presents the key principles for a sustainable, values-based service business.

This unique, insightful and original work will interest scholars and advanced students of marketing, management, organizational behaviour, business ethics, international business and sustainable business.

Bo Edvardsson is professor and Director of CTF-Service Research Center at Karlstad University, Sweden.

Bo Enquist is associate professor at CTF-Service Research Center at Karlstad University, Sweden.

Management, Organizations and Society
Edited by Professor Barbara Czarniawska
Göteborg University, Sweden
and
Professor Martha Feldman
University of Michigan, USA

Management, Organizations and Society presents innovative work grounded in new realities, addressing issues crucial to an understanding of the contemporary world. This is the world of organized societies, where boundaries between formal and informal, public and private, local and global organizations have been displaced or have vanished, along with other nineteenth-century dichotomies and oppositions. Management, apart from becoming a specialized profession for a growing number of people, is an everyday activity for most members of modern societies. Similarly, at the level of enquiry, culture and technology, and literature and economics, can no longer be conceived as isolated intellectual fields; conventional canons and established mainstreams are contested. *Management, Organizations and Society* will address these contemporary dynamics of transformation in a manner that transcends disciplinary boundaries, with work which will appeal to researchers, students and practitioners alike

Other titles in this series:

Contrasting Involvements
A study of management accounting practices in Britain and Germany
Thomas Ahrens

Turning Words, Spinning Worlds
Chapters in organizational ethnography
Michael Rosen

Breaking Through the Glass Ceiling
Women, power and leadership in agricultural organizations
Margaret Alston

The Poetic Logic of Administration
Styles and changes of style in the art of organizing
Kaj Sköldberg

Casting the Other
Maintaining gender inequalities in the workplace
Edited by Barbara Czarniawska and Heather Höpfl

Gender, Identity and the Culture of Organizations
Edited by Iiris Aaltio and Albert J. Mills

Text/Work
Representing organization and organizing representation
Edited by Stephen Lins0tead

The Social Construction of Management
Texts and identities
Nancy Harding

Management Theory
A critical and reflexive reading
Nanette Monin

Values-based services and the co-creation of customer value through values are two fundamental aspects addressed by this book and also an important source of reflection about the need of congruence in today's society.

This book breaks new ground raising two fundamental issues in contemporary service literature: the need and importance of values-based services and the co-creation of customer value through values. It is an essential reading for executives, researchers and students as it provides the basis for reflection about the need of congruence in doing business in today's service society.

Professor Javier Reynoso
Chair, Services Management Research & Education Group
Monterrey Institute of Tecnhology – ITESM Monterrey, Mexico

IKEA is an example of a company with a business idea based on values and innovative approaches to value creation. This book is an analysis of IKEAs value-oriented business and a narrative of the IKEA way of doing things at a strategic as well as tactical level. At the same time it explores the possibilities of adopting a business focus based on service.

Professor Christina Grönroos
Swedish School of Business Administration
and Economics, Helsinki Finland

Through their informed and competent analysis of IKEA's business model, using a service-logic lens, Professors Edvardsson and Enquist provide significant insights into the contextual and collaborative natureof value creation. This book is an important contribution to the ongoing process, in both academics and practice, of shifting from a goods-based to a service-based logic of exchange, marketing, and social responsibility.

Dr Stephen L Vargo
Associate Professor of Marketing,
Shidler College of Business University of Hawaii, USA

Values-based Service for Sustainable Business
Lessons from IKEA

Bo Edvardsson and Bo Enquist

Routledge
Taylor & Francis Group

LONDON AND NEW YORK

First published 2009
by Routledge
2 Park Square, Milton Park, Abingdon, Oxon OX14 4RN

Simultaneously published in the USA and Canada
by Routledge
270 Madison Ave, New York, NY 10016

Routledge is an imprint of the Taylor & Francis Group, an informa business

© 2009 Bo Edvardsson and Bo Enquist

Typeset in Times New Roman by
HWA Text and Data Management, London

British Library Cataloguing in Publication Data
A catalogue record for this book is available from the British Library

Library of Congress Cataloging in Publication Data
Edvardsson, Bo, 1952–
    Values-based service for sustainable business : lessons from IKEA/
    Bo Edvardsson and Bo Enquist.
        p. cm.
    Includes bibliographical references and index.
    1. Service industries. 2. Ikea A/S. 3. Customer services –
    Management. 4. Sustainable development. I. Enquist, Bo. II. Title.
    HD9980.5.E28 2009
    658--dc22   2008021245

ISBN13: 978–0–415–45853–5 (hbk)
ISBN13: 978–0–203–88770–7 (ebk)

ISBN10: 0–415–45853–6 (hbk)
ISBN10: 0–203–88770–0 (ebk)

Contents

Preface

The notion of 'customer value' includes not only *economic value* but also value that is linked to *values*. From the customer's perspective, 'value' is an overall personal assessment of the quality attributes of the market offering in relation to the price and other sacrifices. It is a subjective assessment of the positive and negative consequences associated with the purchase, use and consumption, including values linked to the provider.

Values can be understood as the principles, standards, ethics, and ideals that companies and people live by. A distinction can be made between two main categories of values: (i) a company's *core values* (which form the basis of the company culture); and (ii) *foundation values* (which reflect the norms of society in general). Compliance with the latter category constitutes so-called 'corporate social responsibility' (CSR), which refers to a company's ethical, social and environmental responsibilities. A values-based business is thus based on a combination of core company values and foundation values, which guides the company in creating customer value and a sustainable service business. Such values are crucially important in creating customer value and forming the basis for a sustainable service business.

Mainstream business is today product and production oriented and thus characterised by a 'goods-dominant logic' (GDL), which can be seen as the opposite of a 'service-dominant logic' (SDL). The main focus of the SDL paradigm is that value is co-created with customers and assessed on the basis of 'value in use'. Market offerings are understood as being resources that produce effects. Despite the growing awareness of SDL, the focus in service-management research has continued to be on the structural processes of the service system.

The notion that a service culture, grounded in company core values and CSR, drives service strategy, has not been empirically examined in any great detail. This book focuses on what might be called 'values-based service', with particular emphasis on the role of such service in the furniture company, IKEA. 'Values-based service' is, in this book, defined as service that is firmly based on the core company values as well as social and environmental responsibility. When the core company values, and the social and environmental values are in accordance with the values of customers and other stakeholders, resonance (rather than dissonance) occurs. To be successful, a values-based service business must seek resonance in terms of values, and avoid any suggestion of dissonance. We use narratives from IKEA, together with a conceptual analysis based on SDL to create a framework of values-based service for sustainable business.

This book is the first on the role of values in developing and managing *sustainable* service organisations. The focus of the book is on the role of values in creating customer and shareholder value and thus co-creating a sustainable business. The two basic questions addressed by the book are: (1) What is 'values-based service'? (2) How can values create value for customers and other stakeholders?

Every reflective manager and senior executive can benefit from reading this book. The lessons to be learnt from IKEA are applicable in virtually any organisation. The book is thus useful for managers and executives who are engaged in the areas of marketing, human resources, product and service development, brand management, quality improvement, corporate social responsibility, and customer-relationship management. The book is also intended for MBA and executive MBA programmes at universities, business schools, and institutes, as well as for various other master's programmes at business schools and technical universities.

The first chapter describes and defines values-based service and sustainable business. The chapter also introduces IKEA and notes various dimensions of the company's business model. Chapter 2 provides an overview of the history of IKEA and the social and environmental perspectives that have acted as driving forces for creating economic value. The chapter concludes with a strategic perspective on the values-based culture of IKEA. In Chapter 3, the concept of customer value is discussed, followed by the presentation of this book's framework for how values drive customer value-in-use. With this background, it is possible to conceptualise values-based service in terms of core company values, SDL, CSR to create a sustainable business.

In Chapters 4–6, values-based service thinking is developed within the areas of service experience, service brand, and service leadership. In Chapter 4, the focus is on the service experience and how to make it possible for customers to 'test-drive' services and solutions before purchase and consumption. Chapter 5, which is about values-based service brands and marketing communication, discusses identity, image, and how to 'live the brand'. Chapter 6 is about 'authentic leadership', living the values, and leaders being role models.

Finally in Chapter 7, IKEA is compared with other values-based service companies (such as Starbucks, H&M, and Body Shop) and we present five principles for a sustainable, values-based service business. The overriding orientation of all the companies described here is a genuine focus on the customer. Superior customer value is based on favourable service experiences, a strong brand, and dynamic marketing communication. This requires staying close to the customers, understanding their requirements, and providing solutions that are in accordance with their values and lifestyles. Learning from (and with) customers in various ways is crucially important if a company wishes to remain customer focused.

Corporate social and environmental responsibility has been demonstrated to be profitable – both in the short term and in the long term. Innovative service concepts that utilise physical products as platforms for service and customer experiences can create value in use. The logic of values and the logic of value are synergistic, profitable, and sustainable.

It would have been impossible to carry out this study without support from the KK-foundation in Sweden. This book is part of a research programme at CTF-Service Research Center, Karlstad University. We would like to thank the KK-foundation for financial support, and our colleagues at CTF for continuous support and in particular for feed-back on many versions of the manuscript. We also want to thank the master students who have collected data and visited IKEA stores in many countries and Patrik Edvardsson for assisting us in collecting data. Professor Tore Strandvik from Hanken in Helsinki gave us a number of valuable suggestions how to improve and clarify our findings and the structure of the book. Finally we are most grateful to Marianne Barner and Michael Hay from the IKEA Group and many other executives and co-workers at IKEA around the world who have helped by giving us access to company documents, time for interviews and feed-back on the manuscript (see Appendix 2). This completely independent research has been carried out without any financial support or directions from IKEA.

Bo Edvardsson and Bo Enquist
Karlstad, May 2008

1 Setting the stage

Introduction

Value creation is a multi-faceted and important area for both scholars and managers. Value for customers of a *product* (for example, a car) is created in a somewhat different manner than it is for customers of a *service* (for example, a transportation solution). In the first case, a so-called 'goods logic' is required to understand value production, whereas, in the second case, the transportation solution needs a 'service logic' to describe and understand the customer value being created. The essential difference between 'goods logic' and 'service logic' is that the former perceives value as being embedded in physical products during manufacturing, whereas the latter holds that value is co-created with the customer and is experienced and assessed when the service is utilised within the customer's own context.

The notion of 'customer value' includes not only *economic value* but also value that is related to *values* (in the sense of 'ideals'). From the customer's perspective, value is an overall personal assessment of the quality attributes of the market offering in relation to the price and other sacrifices. It is a subjective assessment of the positive and negative consequences associated with the purchase (Woodruff, 1997), including values linked to the provider. From the company's point of view, the buying motives are the basis for a customer value proposition, which makes it a strategic issue in terms of service development, segmentation, and marketing communication (Rintamäki *et al.*, 2007).

Values can be understood as the principles, standards, ethics, and ideals that companies (and people) live by (Waddock and Bodwell, 2007). A distinction can be made between two main categories of values: (i) a company's *core values* (which form the basis of the company culture); and (ii) *foundation values* (which reflect the norms of society in general). Compliance with the latter category constitutes so-called 'corporate social responsibility' (CSR), which refers to a company's social and environmental responsibilities. A values-based business is thus based on a combination of core company values and foundation values, which guides the company in creating customer value and a sustainable service business.

Such values are crucially important in creating customer value and forming the basis for a sustainable service business. For example, an important quality attribute of a car is its engine power; the more power it has for the same price, the better value it represents. However, this notion of 'value' might conflict with a customer's personal values – that a more powerful car will cause more damage to the environment than a less powerful model. In these circumstances, a car with the same engine power but greater environmental 'friendliness' would be seen as having greater customer value. It is thus apparent that values in the sense of 'ideals') contribute to customers' perception of the value of attributes possessed by goods and services.

Relatively little attention has been devoted by scholars and practitioners to this important role played by values in creating value for customers and other stakeholders. Service management has focused on other areas – such as service offering, service quality, service encounters, technology in service, complaints management, service recovery, new service development, service competition, service strategy, and so on. However, more recently, the implications of the so-called 'service-dominant logic' (SDL) (Vargo and Lusch, 2004; Lusch and Vargo, 2006) have become a subject of greater interest. Mainstream business thinking is today product and production oriented and thus characterised by a 'goods-dominant logic' (GDL) (ibid.), which can be seen as the opposite of SDL. The main focus of the SDL paradigm is that value is co-created with customers and assessed on the basis of 'value-in-use'. Market offerings (physical products and services) are understood as being resources that produce effects. Customers thus use their knowledge and skills when service value is created and assessed – for example, when using a mobile phone to communicate.

Despite the growing awareness of SDL, the focus in service-management research has continued to be on the structural processes of the service system, which is part of the business model. A definition of the concept 'business model' from a GDL point of view suggested by Osterwalder *et al.* (2005, p. 3) is as follows:

> A business model is a conceptual tool that contains a big set of elements and their relationships and allows expressing the business logic of a specific firm. It is a description of the value a company offers to one or several segments of customers and the architecture of the firm and its network of partners for creating, marketing, and delivering this value

and relationship capital, to generate profitable and sustainable revenue streams.

Our business model thinking is related to SDL and thus emphasises value-in-use and co-creation of customer value and values resonance, which we will later introduce as a label for a synergy between corporate values, foundation values and customer values.

The notion that a service culture, grounded in company core values and CSR, drives service strategy, has not been empirically examined in any great detail. This book focuses on what might be called 'values-based service', with particular emphasis on the role of such service in the furniture company, IKEA. 'Values-based service' is, in this book, defined as service that is firmly based on the core company values as well as social and environmental responsibility. When the core company values, the social and environmental values are in accordance with the values of customers and other stakeholders, resonance (rather than dissonance) occurs. To be successful, a values-based service business must seek resonance in terms of values, and avoid any suggestion of dissonance; that is, the firm and its stakeholders must have *shared values*. As Pruzan (1998, p. 1380) observed:

> Business and public leaders are realising that good answers to complex questions can be found by supplementing the narrow language of efficiency, control and profit with multidimensional and qualitative measures that explicitly recognise the values the organisation shares with its stakeholders.

In accordance with the SDL paradigm outlined above, value can be understood as being *co-created* (Normann and Ramirez, 1998) through strong relationships with stakeholders (Gummesson, 2007). The key stakeholder in this book is the customer, and value-in-use is understood within the context of the customers' needs and values. Other stakeholders worthy of consideration are the shareholders, suppliers, employees, media, partners, and non-governmental organisations (NGOs).

This book uses narratives from IKEA, together with a conceptual analysis based on SDL, and a values-based business model to create a framework of values-based service for sustainable business. IKEA was founded by Ingvar Kamprad in 1943 as a one-man mail-order furniture company in a farm village in Småland, southern Sweden. What might be called the 'IKEA concept' really began in the 1950s with a showroom where customers could see and touch the products, and the catalogue and the store support one another. From the beginning, the focus of IKEA was on function, quality, and low price, and these continue to be the core values of the firm, although good design has been added as a fourth core value. IKEA has become a fast-growing, global, home-furnishing group with 273 stores in 40 countries (as of February 2008). In the year ending 30 August 2007, IKEA had a turnover of 182 billion Swedish crowns (US$29 billion) and 522 million visitors to the business. IKEA's research has revealed that the average customer returns to an IKEA store four times a year.

Aims and objectives of the book

This book is the first on the role of values in developing and managing *sustainable* service organisations. The focus of the book is on the role of values in creating customer and shareholder value and thus co-creating a sustainable business. The two basic questions addressed by the book are:

• What is 'values-based service'?
• How can values create value for customers and other stakeholders?

Values can contribute to value-in-use for customers or they can diminish value. Attractive corporate values that resonate with the personal values of customers can build a business, whereas values that create dissonance with customers' values are likely to drive customers away.

In examining these ideas in a practical business situation, it was important to choose a service company that has been successful in terms of growth and profitability. Some might argue that IKEA is a product retailer and not a service company; however, IKEA views itself as a service provider – because the company's focus is not on the furniture itself but on 'solutions to real-life problems' and making a contribution to a 'better life' for the majority of people. This is clearly a service concept in which the physical products are perceived as platforms for service experiences that create customer value. Moreover, IKEA is a service-oriented company in the sense that the focus of the company is clearly on *serving* people with well-designed, quality products at a price they can afford.

IKEA has been, over the long term, a very profitable company that has become the global leader in its industry. The firm is known for a strong service culture that emphasises company core values and a strong sense of corporate and social responsibility. IKEA has demonstrated an ability to serve customers and renew its business at a time when many other companies have been more focused on narrow conceptions of shareholder value and internal issues. Other companies and organisations can learn from IKEA, and it is the aim of this book to provide inspiration and practical guidance in analysing an organisation's values as a basis for a sustainable service business. In short, this book contributes to a better understanding of the strategic role of values in forming and directing service strategy and value-in-use for customers.

Target readership

Every reflective manager and senior executive can benefit from reading this book. The lessons to be learnt from IKEA are applicable in virtually any organisation. In particular, other firms can learn from IKEA's long-term commitment to serving the majority of people, its global perspective, and its dynamic values-based culture that supports and directs the mission, strategy, business model, market offerings, and development of the IKEA brand. The book is thus useful for managers and executives who are engaged in the areas of marketing, human resources, product and service development, brand management, quality improvement, corporate social responsibility, and customer-relationship management. The book is also intended for MBA and executive MBA programmes at universities, business schools, and institutes, as well as for various other master's programmes at business schools and technical universities.

Structure of the book

The first three chapters of this book provide a basis for a more in-depth exploration of the issues involved. The first chapter describes and defines values-based service and sustainable business. The chapter also introduces IKEA and notes various dimensions of the company's business model. Chapter 2 provides an overview of the history of IKEA and the social and environmental perspectives that have acted as driving forces for creating economic value. The chapter concludes with a strategic perspective on the values-based culture of IKEA. In Chapter 3, the concept of customer value is discussed, followed by the presentation of this book's framework for how values drive customer value-in-use. With this background, it is possible to conceptualise values-based service in terms of core company values, SDL, CSR, to create a sustainable business.

In Chapters 4–6, values-based service thinking is developed within the areas of service experience, service brand, and service leadership. In Chapter 4, the focus is on the service experience and how to make it possible for customers to 'test-drive' services and solutions before purchase and consumption. Chapter 5, which is about values-based service brands and marketing communication, discusses identity, image, and how to 'live the brand'. Chapter 6 is about 'authentic leadership', living the values, and leaders being role models. Finally in Chapter 7, IKEA is compared with other values-based service companies (such as Starbucks, H&M, and Body Shop); from this analysis, the book presents five principles for a sustainable, values-based service business.

IKEA as a values-based company for sustainable business

Values-based businesses in general

The values of a company guide the business model, the attitudes and behaviours of the firm's leaders, employees, and customers, as well as determining the business strategy and vision of the company. In the context of this book, such values (in the sense of 'ideals') are crucial for understanding customer value and value-in-use.

Costa and Bjelland (2006) made the following observation about the importance of corporate values:

> ... chief executives take extreme risks, diversifying from their core businesses, betting on untried technologies, acquiring companies in unrelated sectors – [in short], doing whatever they can to deliver revenue growth and bolster their stock. In this environment, executives ignore their company's core values at their peril. The absence of values-based decision-making ... is one of the common failings of ... departed executives. It is leading to a polarization between those companies that continue to succeed by remaining true to those values and those that are exposed by diversifying too far, too fast.

Figure 1.1 presents this problem in terms of a matrix of two value-creation logics (service-dominant logic and goods-dominant logic) on the vertical axis and two business models (a control-based business model and a values-based business model) on the horizontal axis. The term 'control-based business model' refers to a short-term focus on financial results, whereas the 'values-based business model' shifts the focus from a short-term preoccupation with financial matters to incorporate long-term, values-driven governance principles and key performance indicators. In such a 'values-based business model', the core company values, foundation values (that is, the company's social and environmental responsibilities), and customer values drive the financial and other business goals (such as growth, customer satisfaction, and risk). By combining a service-dominant logic with a values-based business model, a company positions itself in the upper-right section of the matrix shown in Figure 1.1. It is the contention of this book that this position facilitates a sustainable values-based service business.

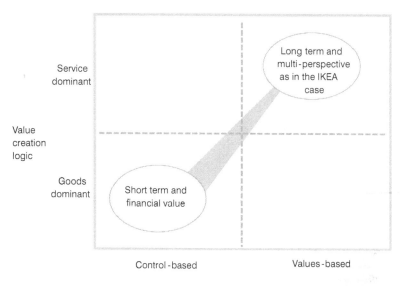

Figure 1.1   Value creation logic and business models

IKEA as a values-based service company

The term 'IKEA Way' is an expression that encapsulates IKEA's approach to doing things in a values-based manner, which is rooted in the history and heritage of the company. A story from IKEA (below) illustrates what is meant by the 'IKEA Way'.

The core company values and foundation values of IKEA form the basis of a strong service culture that is illustrated in the following quotation from the president and CEO of IKEA, Anders Dahlvig (as quoted in Kling and Goteman, 2003, p. 36):

> Culture has to ... support the business idea or the strategy that the company has. The culture is a very important part of a company in the sense that the values of the culture really influence the business itself. I think it is pretty logical and transparent in our company ... cost consciousness, for example ... is an important value that I think we should have ... it is our strategy to be a low-price company... The difficulty is to make people act cost-consciously even in times when the economy is strong.

The 'IKEA Way'

This is a story about a company that did everything wrong. Right from the beginning we did the complete opposite of what you might read in the books on 'how to succeed in business'. Instead of analysing the market and finding out people's shopping behaviour, we started looking for skilled manufacturers. Instead of planning clever marketing plans, we went looking for good raw materials that we knew we could turn into good-quality furniture. We figured that we liked and needed the furniture we made, so why wouldn't others? And because our manufacturers, the down-to-earth ordinary people who actually made the furniture, liked the furniture – why wouldn't others? This straightforward approach to the furniture business, which developed furniture by starting at the 'wrong' end, gave us two huge advantages. First, our manufacturers and our product developers figured out how to maximise the use of raw materials and production processes while simultaneously fulfilling people's needs and preferences. Second, the costs became exceptionally low. Now, if your costs are exceptionally low, you can do two things. You can sell your goods for as high a price as possible (which is what most companies do, of course), or you can sell at the lowest-possible price (which is what no-one does – at least until we entered the scene). By reading our story, understanding our vision, and sharing the values behind our business idea, you will understand why doing it all 'wrong' is actually the 'right' way to do it!

Adapted from Inter IKEA Systems BV (1999)

IKEA's vision, business idea, and strategy

IKEA's *vision* is 'to create a better everyday life for the majority of people'. The company's *business idea* is 'to offer a wide range of well-designed, functional home-furnishing products at prices so low that as many people as possible will be able to afford them'. IKEA provides smart solutions for homes by implementing three criteria: good design, functionality, and low price (IKEA of Sweden, 1995).

In a narrow sense, strategy-making is concerned with the positioning of an organisation in appropriate market niches; in a broader sense, it refers to how the collective resources, structure, and culture of an organisation establish (and, when necessary, change) its basic orientation. Strategy-

making thus involves more than planning; it is integrally concerned with
vision and ideals.

Strategies are not only plans for the future, but also patterns of norms
and values from the past. Strategic leaders are thus 'craftsmen' whose task
is to create a strategy from a past of corporate capabilities with a view
to a future of market opportunities (and threats). Professional craftsmen
bring to the task their knowledge of past experience and the resources at
hand to create a strategy that is likely to produce good outcomes. This is
the essence of crafting a strategy. Strategic leadership is aware of what
constitutes the 'soul' of the organisation, what is important to customers,
what is occurring in service performance, and what should be done to
improve it. Effective strategic leaders put all of this together in crafting a
service strategy that provides a basis for establishing an overall strategic
direction.

Berry (1995, p. 62) has this to say about a service strategy:

> All great service companies have a clear, compelling service strategy.
> They have a 'reason for being' that energizes the organization and
> defines the word 'service'. With a clear, compelling service strategy,
> decision makers know better which initiatives to approve and which to
> reject; the strategy is the guide. With a clear, compelling service strategy,
> service providers know better how to serve customers; the strategy is
> the guide. Thick policy-and-procedures manuals are unneeded.

IKEA's store concept

IKEA stores have a strict structure, which systematically reflects the
company values. In every section of the stores, customers are presented
with selected products with a large price tag showing a low price. At the
entrance to every store there is a playroom for children, where parents can
leave their children under supervision of IKEA employees, free of charge.
Every store features a 'living room' near the entrance, where customers
are shown examples of how to decorate their homes. Various parts of these
rooms have certain customer segments in mind and have different themes
– such as 'young Swedish', 'Scandinavian style', and 'modern style'. If an
IKEA outlet wishes to organise its particular store in another way it has to
obtain permission from head office.

The concept of the stores is designed to encourage people to stay and
browse through the huge departments, and many customers buy items
that they had not planned to purchase when they initially decided to visit
the store. Many people go because of the cheap food and many Swedish
delicacies that are on sale.

The uniformity of the store concept ensures that the names of the products are the same everywhere in the world and that the unique brand of IKEA is retained in every store. However, the mix of items that are offered for sale can differ, depending on the local market. Such 'localisation' is achieved through a combination of a 'base range' (that is, a range of products that all IKEA stores carry) and an 'extra range' (that is, a range of products that a store carries, depending on local requirements).

The IKEA business concept can be summarised in the following ten points (as adapted from an interview with the CEO of IKEA, Anders Dahlvig, reported in Kling and Goteman, 2003):

- Rather than boutique stores in city centres, IKEA developed large stores on the outskirts of cities.
- In other stores, someone serves the customers when they come in; in IKEA's stores, customers serve themselves.
- Most businesses source their products domestically; IKEA sources globally.
- Most furniture businesses target middle-aged (or older) people, whereas IKEA focuses on younger people and young families.
- Rather than dark, heavy furniture, which was often the case in other furniture businesses, IKEA introduced a lighter Scandinavian style.
- In other stores, furniture is assembled and delivered to the customer; in IKEA it is purchased in packs, and the customer assembles it.
- The IKEA values and the Swedish heritage are an important basis for the brand.
- IKEA does not own the means of production; rather, IKEA has purchasing agreements for 90 per cent of its stock, which gives the firm greater flexibility.
- In general, IKEA buys land and builds its store on it. This means that IKEA can control costs (such as rent). In addition, it gains advantages from gradual increases in the value of its properties.
- Corporate social responsibility and sustainable business are both emphasised in IKEA.

The IKEA brand

According to an article in *Business Week* by Capell (2005), IKEA is 'a world of contemporary design, low prices, and wacky promotions'. He (ibid., p. 46) described IKEA in the following terms:

> IKEA has become the curator of people's lifestyles, if not their lives. At a time when consumers face so many choices for everything they buy, IKEA provides a one-stop sanctuary for coolness.

In markets where IKEA is active, the firm has a market share of approximately 5–10 per cent; however, according to the CEO, Anders Dahlvig: 'The awareness of our brand is much bigger than the size of our company' (Capell, 2005, p. 47).

Questions

1 Do companies have values?
2 If companies do have values, how can business leaders manage these values?
3 How (and how much) do the values influence company performance and results?
4 Are some values theoretical 'ideals' whereas others are pragmatic and achievable?
5 Should companies strive for homogeneous values or diverse values?
6 Are some values (or constellations of values) more profitable than others?

References

Berry, L.L. (1995) *On Great Service*. New York: Free Press.
Capell, K. (2005) How the Swedish retailer became a global cult brand, *Business Week*, November 14, cover story.
Costa, K. and Bjelland, O. (2006) *Wall Street Journal* online, 28 December 2006.
Edvardsson, B. and Enquist, B. (2002) 'The IKEA Saga': how service culture drives service strategy, *The Service Industries Journal*, vol. 22, No. 4, pp. 153–86.
Grönroos, C. (2007) *In Search of a New Logic for Marketing: Foundations of Contemporary Theory*. Chichester: John Wiley & Sons.
Gummesson, E. (2007) Exit services marketing – enter service marketing, *Journal of Customer Behaviour*, Vol. 6, No. 2, pp. 113–41.
IKEA (2007) Online. Available HTTP: www.ikea.com (accessed 4 June 2007).
IKEA of Sweden (1995) *Democratic Design*, booklet published by IKEA of Sweden, Älmhult, Sweden to mark IKEA's 50th jubilee.
Kling, K. and Goteman, I. (2003) IKEA CEO Anders Dahlvig on international growth and IKEA's unique corporate culture and brand identity, *Academy of Management Executive*, Vol. 17, No. 1, pp. 31–7.
Lusch, R.F, and Vargo. S.L. (eds) (2006) *The Service-Dominant Logic of Marketing*. New York: M.E. Sharpe.
Normann, R. and Ramirez, R. (1998) *Designing Interactive Strategy from Value Chain to Value Constellation*. Chichester: John Wiley & Sons (second edition).
Osterwalder, A., Pigneur, Y. and Tucci, C.L. (2005) Clarifying business models: origins, present, and future of the concept, *Communications of the Association for Information Systems*, Vol. 16, No. 3, pp. 1–25.
Pettigrew, A.M. (1979) On studying organizational cultures, *Administrative Science Quarterly*, December, Vol. 24.

Pruzan, P. (1998) From control to values based management and accountability, *Journal of Business Ethics*, Vol. 17, pp. 1379–94.

Rintamäki, T., Kuusela, H. and Mitronen, L. (2007) Identifying competitive customer value propositions in retailing, *Managing Service Quality*, Vol. 17, No. 6, pp. 621–34.

Torekull, B. (1999) *Leading by Design: The IKEA Story*. New York: Harper Business.

Vargo, S.L. and Lusch, R.F. (2004) Evolving to a new dominant logic of marketing, *Journal of Marketing*, Vol. 68, January, pp. 1–17.

Vargo, S.L. and Lusch, R.F. (2008) Service-dominant logic: continuing the evolution, *Journal of the Academy of Marketing Science* (online version).

Waddock, S. and Bodwell, C. (2007) *Total Responsibility Management: The Manual*. Sheffield: Greenleaf Publishing.

Woodruff, R.B. (1997) Customer value: the next source for competitive advantage, *Journal of the Academy of Marketing Science*, Vol. 25, No. 2, pp. 139–53.

2 Sustainable business embedded in history and heritage

Introduction

In a globalised world economy, supplier chains have promoted a phenomenon of so-called 'commoditization' (Friedman, 2005, p. 344), whereby all processes became standardised (and often digitalised), and available to many players. Although this can lead to lower prices and convenience, the dark side of the phenomenon is that there is scope for manipulation and exploitation. In the case of IKEA, the process of 'commoditization' emphasises better quality at lower prices, with sustainable environmental and social standards. IKEA has thus created a business case for the new globalised economy, in which costs are cut without sacrificing quality or stringent social and environmental standards (Konzelmann *et al.*, 2005).

IKEA is an example of what the president and CEO of IBM, Samuel J. Palmisano, has called a 'globally integrated enterprise' (Palmisano, 2006). According to Palmisano (2006), businesses are changing in fundamental ways – *structurally*, *operationally*, and *culturally* – in response to globalisation and new technology; as a result, the larger companies are no longer 'multinational corporations' (MNCs), but *globally integrated enterprises*. Palmisano (2006) has pointed out that globally integrated enterprises can deliver enormous economic benefits to both developed and developing countries. He has also talked about 'global collaboration', whereby various stakeholders interact in development and learning processes.

This chapter describes a good business example of a 'globally integrated enterprise' in the case of IKEA, in which economic, environmental, and social perspectives are integrated and support one another. The supply chain of IKEA has its roots in the Swedish county of Småland, which is a region of limited resources, and this represented a significant challenge for the management of IKEA in its entrepreneurial efforts to create smart solutions (Edvardsson and Enquist, 2002).

Foundation: the entrepreneur and his testament

IKEA was founded by Ingvar Kamprad in 1943 as a one-man mail-order furniture company in a farm village in Småland, southern Sweden. Kamprad had (and maintains) a dream of 'good capitalism' (as recorded by Torekull (1998, p. 153):

> The question is whether, as an entrepreneur, I can combine ... a profit-making business with a lasting human social vision. I like to think that it must be possible. I don't mean to say that capitalism can avoid fiascos. I myself have been the cause of several. To fail is part of all evolution. But every day, IKEA strives to develop and achieve a better future for the people, our customers. A company goal of that kind influences those working toward it. Studies show that people who work for IKEA believe that they really are working for a better society and that they therefore like working for IKEA. They believe that in their daily lives they are contributing to a better world.

Similarly, Anders Moberg, who succeeded Kamprad as president and CEO of IKEA, has argued that IKEA's principles of social responsibility are reflected in 'trade with responsibility'; according to Moberg, 'trade is better than aid'. As recorded in Edvardsson and Enquist (2002, p. 170), Moberg had this to say about IKEA's role:

> I'm convinced that cross-border cooperation leads to development. Hundreds of thousands of workers in our suppliers' factories depend on the fact that IKEA assumes a responsible attitude to its long-term commitments. We create employment, we open markets for these people's products, and we work together with our suppliers to make constant improvements. IKEA is a commercial company, but there is a social side to our vision and our business idea. Only by being open and honest can we create the right conditions to keep improving everyday life for the majority of people.

The strong culture of IKEA is based on shared values and meanings, and Kamprad's 'Testament of a Furniture Dealer' (see Appendix 1) is of great importance in stating these values and meanings in creating a better everyday life for the majority of people. Kamprad put it this way in the 'Testament':

> Once and for all we ... decided to side with the many. What is good for our customers is also good for us in the long run. This is an objective that entails responsibility.

The 'Testament' is divided into nine subsections as follows: (i) 'The Product Range: Our Identity'; (ii) 'The IKEA Spirit: a Strong and Living Reality'; (iii) 'Profit Gives us Resources'; (iv) 'To Reach Good Results with Small Means'; (v) 'Simplicity is a Virtue'; (vi) 'The Different Way'; (vii) 'Concentration of Energy: Important to Our Success'; (viii) 'To Assume Responsibility: a Privilege'; and (ix) 'Most Things Still Remain To Be Done: a Glorious Future!'.

In February 1996, Kamprad produced a second edition of his 'Testament'. The second edition was supplemented with particular words and phrases that were seen as being important in the IKEA heritage. These words included: 'humility', 'will power'; 'simplicity'; 'the majority of people'; 'making do'; 'experience'; 'thinking differently'; 'never say never'; 'the IKEA way'; 'honesty'; 'common sense'; 'cost-consciousness'; 'accepting and delegating responsibility'; 'facing up to reality'; 'solidarity'; and 'enthusiasm'. Of these phrases, 'the majority of people' is especially important to IKEA's vision. Kamprad made the following comments about this aspect of his 'Testament' (Edvardsson and Enquist, 2002, p. 167):

> We have decided to stand on the side of the majority of people, which involves taking on more responsibility than might at first seem to be the case. Standing on the side of the majority of people means representing the interests of ordinary people, no matter whether that is good or bad for our own short-term interests. It means getting rid of designs that are difficult and expensive to produce, even if they are easy to sell. It means refusing to sell in hard currency to consumers in a country with non-convertible currencies – even though that would make our profits bigger and our problems fewer. Developing a range and presenting it in an imaginative, appealing way in all our stores demands a great deal of knowledge about the lives, hopes, and aspirations of the majority of people. The best way to learn this is through personal experience – not as tourists gaping at things with cameras slung around our necks. Using public transport is one good way of getting closer to people.

With regard to 'cost-consciousness', Kamprad made the following observations (Edvardsson and Enquist, 2002, p. 168):

> This notion is probably the easiest to understand, because it goes hand in hand with our business idea. Our low prices are written into our business idea as an essential condition for our success. Anyone can tell you that it is impossible to have a low price, good quality, and good profitability if you don't have low costs. So cost-consciousness

has to permeate everything we do – almost to the point of that kind of exaggerated meanness that others call 'penny-pinching'.

Innovative business and social consciousness

Adam Morgan, in his book *The Pirate Inside*, related a story from the early days of IKEA when Kamprad was in the habit of going into wood factories to look at the 'off cuts' (the timber to be thrown away as waste) and asking himself what furniture could be produced from such 'waste'. According to Morgan (2004, p. 19): 'He knew by taking materials that were not just cheap, but of no value to the current owner, [that] he could produce not just well-priced products but extraordinarily priced products'. Morgan called this kind of insight 'outlooking' – by which he meant the ability to think differently and to see things that no-one else could see.

Kamprad continues to have a role as a 'senior advisor' to IKEA. In that role he is able to speak freely as part of a sense-making process of creating 'shared meanings' in re-producing the strong IKEA culture. According to Torekull (1998, p. 211):

> He asks a thousand questions, exhorts, provokes, lets go, but comes back, encourages with a single friendly word, demolishes with a random word, hugs, kisses, and irritates with his presence. He is thrifty, sometimes thoughtless and abrupt, but towards friends he is warm and generous. He bombards his people with a thousand ideas from a bottomless store, thoughts crowding in, clamouring to get out, to be realized before he says thanks and good-bye.

The IKEA saga

In her doctoral thesis about the IKEA culture, Salzer (1994, p. 61) made the following observation:

> The corporate saga of IKEA is ... not only a vivid and heroic story of how IKEA ... started and grew into a successful international group; it is also a story that reflects how ... IKEA looks at itself and its role in the world. It reflects its special language, its myths, and its heroes.

In their article, 'The IKEA Saga: How Service Culture Drives Service Strategy', Edvardsson and Enquist (2002) presented the 'IKEA saga' in three 'Acts'.

• Act I: The creation of IKEA and its concepts

- Act II: Searching for 'eternal life' for IKEA
- Act III: A new IKEA generation takes over

Act I: The creation of IKEA and its concepts

Act I tells three stories of how core IKEA concepts came into being. This Act is about: (i) the notion of 'catalogue and store as one unit'; (ii) the first self-assembled furniture; and (iii) how Poland became the key for low-cost production. The story of self-assembled furniture is of great importance for IKEA. Kamprad tells how the whole idea started. He talks about himself and Gillis Lundgren who was at that time a young draftsman at an advertising agency:

> That was the beginning of designing our own furniture, essentially avoiding the boycott and its problems. But on one occasion when we had photographed a table and were to pack it up again afterward, it was Gillis who muttered something like 'God, what a lot of space it takes up. Let's take the legs off and put them under the tabletop.' The one fine day – or was it a night? – we had our first flat parcel, and thus we started a revolution. In the 1953 catalog, which was ready in 1952, 'Max,' the very first self-assembled table, was included. After that followed a whole series of other self-assembled furniture, and by 1956 the concept was more or less systematized. (Torekull, 1999, p. 52)

Act II: Searching for 'eternal life' for IKEA

Act II tells stories about creating a company for 'eternal life', a period of international expansion, and a later period of consolidation. Narratives of important events in IKEA history at this time included the problems that the company had in North America before it became profitable and the complexities of the notions of 'good capitalism' and 'trade with responsibility'.

An important aspect of the expansion of IKEA to become a global company has been its independence and the desire of Kamprad to seek so-called 'eternal life' for his company. Torekull (1998, p. 97) explained the notion of 'eternal life' for the firm as follows:

> When Ingvar Kamprad decided to go abroad, his ambition was ... to give his lifework the best possible chance of 'eternal life'. Long after he passed away, he wanted the company to be able to develop and flourish. In his own words: 'As long as there is human housing on our earth, there will be a need for a strong and efficient IKEA'. But his ambition

went further than that. No one and nothing was to destroy or endanger his business vision, whether a member of the family or market forces, or politicians. Barriers were to be constructed not only against hostile assaults but also against the danger [of] apathy ... IKEA was a concept to be protected in the event of war and subversive political changes. And power – that was ultimately to lead back to the family in the future as well.

The solution was that IKEA was to be governed by a 'double command' structure. Torekull (1998) described: (i) the 'spirit' (which takes care of the concept); and (ii) the 'hand' (which takes care of the operations). Inter IKEA Systems BV (a holding company in Luxembourg) is the owner and franchiser of the IKEA concept. This holding company has a coordination office in Brussels (Belgium). Some IKEA retailers worldwide operate on a franchise basis. Most IKEA retailers belong to the IKEA Group (the 'hand'), which consists of a large number of companies supported by nine staff units located in the Netherlands (IKEA Services BV) and Sweden (IKEA Services AB).

Act III: A new IKEA generation takes over

In 1999, a press release from IKEA announced the appointment of new leadership for IKEA. The press release read as follows (Edvardsson and Enquist, 2002, p. 170):

The Board has appointed Anders Dahlvig as new President of the IKEA Group, and he will, together with Hans Gydell, lead IKEA into the future. Anders Moberg has, after almost thirty years within IKEA, [including] almost half the time as its President, decided to accept new challenges outside the company.

This represented a generational change in the IKEA saga. But the original founder, Ingvar Kamprad, continued to act as a senior advisor for IKEA. Twenty years after he produced his 'Testament', Kamprad published a document known as the 'IKEA Values' (see box). These values represent guidelines for the new generation of IKEA leaders in the third millennium.

IKEA values

Togetherness and enthusiasm: We respect each other's efforts. We realise that we all need each other. Everyone is prepared to lend a hand.

Constant desire for renewal: A willingness to make change in a constant search for smarter solutions.

Cost consciousness: Achieving good results with small resources. Never producing a product or a service without a price tag. Awareness of the little expenses that can easily mount up. It is impossible to have a low price if you don't have a low cost. An awareness that time is money.

Willingness to accept and delegate responsibility: We must always be more than willing to accept and to delegate responsibility. Making mistakes now and again is the privilege of dynamic co-workers – they are the ones who have the ability to put things right. We encourage those who have the desire and the courage to take responsibility.

Humility and willpower: The way people behave towards other people and their ideas. Consideration, respect, friendliness, generosity, sincerity, admitting your mistakes, listening to others – these are the qualities we like to encourage at IKEA. A question of taking responsibility, making the decisions, and having the courage to act.

Simplicity: Simple habits and simple actions are part of IKEA, but we must never forget to show respect for each other.

Leadership by example: Set a good example by your behaviour and thereby create a feeling of well-being and a good working environment.

Daring to be different: 'Why not?' or 'Is there another way of doing this?' We encourage our co-workers to come up with unconventional ideas and to dare to try them out. At IKEA it's always possible to test new, exciting ideas within the framework of our concept.

Striving to meet reality: Maintaining practical connections with daily activities.

The importance of constantly being on the way: This means being stimulated by finding ways of achieving the goal than by the goal itself. Constantly asking ourselves whether what we are doing today can be done better tomorrow.

No fear of making mistakes: To allow people to get things wrong now and again. To encourage initiative, but with the privilege of making mistakes and putting them right afterwards.

Adapted from Inter IKEA Systems BV.

The IKEA saga from an environmental perspective

The environmental aspects of the IKEA saga are worthy of special note. IKEA (2005, p. 4) had this to say about its long-standing commitment to environmental issues:

> Ever since IKEA was founded in 1943, we have tried hard to avoid wasting resources – everything from natural resources to other resources such as time and money. This approach is essential in order to produce and sell home furnishings at low prices while reducing environmental impact.

Despite its early commitment to environmental protection, IKEA encountered a serious environmental issue in the mid-1980s when Denmark established a new law regulating the maximum emissions allowed from 'formaldehyde off-gassing' in the production of particle board, which was, at that time, a core component of many IKEA products. The issue was quickly referred to IKEA's quality department, and the firm immediately established a large testing laboratory for its products. That laboratory later became one of the most sophisticated environmental-testing facilities in Scandinavia.

IKEA also received criticism for its packaging waste, and especially for its use of PVC plastic (which had become a controversial issue in Germany). There was also criticism of IKEA's long-established catalogue, which had achieved the largest circulation of any colour catalogue in the world; critics questioned the number of trees that were felled each year for pulp to make the catalogue's paper, and the use of chlorine in bleaching the pulp. The company was also criticised for the amount of waste produced in the making of the catalogues and for the waste created by discarded catalogues after use. At the time, these environmental issues were new and confusing for the company, but IKEA began to recognise that environmental concern was a new market reality.

In 1992, IKEA faced yet another 'formaldehyde crisis'. This involved IKEA's largest market, Germany, and concerned one of its biggest-selling items – the popular 'Billy bookshelf', which represented millions of dollars of revenue per annum for the company. By the time of this crisis, IKEA management had already agreed (in 1990) that environmental issues were becoming of major importance to the firm's business. The company therefore adopted its first environmental policy for a one-year trial period. In 1991, IKEA's board approved the current IKEA environmental policy.

Since the formal adoption of a long-term environmental policy in 1991, IKEA has been working systematically to cope with a variety of environmental and social issues. To mark the 50th anniversary of IKEA in the mid-1990s, IKEA published a booklet entitled 'Democratic Design'. In the final chapter of this booklet, Viktor Papanek, an architect from the University of Kansas School of Architecture and Urban Design, made the following observations (Papanek, 1995, pp. 255–6):

> ... the future of IKEA ... will be closely linked to ecology and the environment ... During the past four years, IKEA has ... implemented an ecologically responsible and environmentally friendly programme throughout its design, manufacturing, and distribution channels ... policies that protect the rainforest hardwoods and certain shellacs, reassess the concept of responsibility packaging, provide training for workers, and promote the development of pleasant working condition. And this is just a start. I can see IKEA re-examining the life-cycle of their products ... with a view towards making their furniture 'long-life', and taking into account the final disassembly stage to make recycling easier.

These comments were prophetic in predicting how IKEA would work to develop its program of social and environmental responsibility as an integrated part of its business model. IKEA's long-term orientation is to have a minimal impact on the environment while creating a better everyday life for as many people as possible.

John Elkington, a former chairman of SustainAbility, a UK-based consultancy firm on environmental issues, has worked with many leading global companies in helping them to perceive sustainability as a business opportunity. In his provocative book, *Cannibals with Forks* (Elkington, 1997), he developed the notion of a 'triple bottom line' – which encourages companies to take proper account of *three* dimensions (economic, environmental, and social) in working towards a corporate 'bottom line'. In this book, Elkington (1997, p. 262) made the following observations about Kamprad and IKEA:

> Another entrepreneur who has tried to build his company to last is Ingvar Kamprad, founder of IKEA, the giant furniture and house-wares

business. Far from coincidentally, the company has a well-developed environmental conscience. 'I don't want to take personal credit for our environmental credits,' said Kamprad. But, he noted, 'If your goal is to serve people in general, then you know they are very interested in a sound situation in the environment ... We have worked many years to build a long-lasting enterprise in many countries ... Shareholders want short-term rewards. They demand annual profits and a rising pattern of earnings. That is against my way of thinking.' As a result, IKEA has rejected any public sale of shares.

Social and environmental responsibility for sustainable business

As a result of the developments described above, IKEA is now working systematically to create a more sustainable environment for all its stakeholders and for future generations of stakeholders. This can be understood as part of the company's service-quality improvement processes and represents a natural part of the IKEA business model (Enquist *et al.*, 2007). Waddock and Bodwell (2007) compared this approach with total quality management (TQM) and coined the term 'total responsibility management' (TRM).

Social and environmental strategy

The 'IWAY' is the code of conduct developed and introduced by IKEA in 2000. IWAY emphasises good working conditions for employees and suppliers, and the protection of the outside environment. IKEA obliges all of its suppliers to comply with national laws and international conventions concerning the protection of the environment, and to provide healthy and safe working conditions for all staff members. This policy is part of IKEA's commitment to *sustainable business*. Anders Dahlvig, the president and CEO of the IKEA Group, explained the firm's thinking regarding social and environmental responsibility in a 'President's message' to stakeholders in 2005 (see box).

Co-workers

IKEA prefers to talk about 'co-workers' rather than 'employees'. The term 'co-worker' better reflects the IKEA way of doing business. It suggests shared values, such as togetherness, cost-consciousness, respect, and simplicity.

IKEA is a worldwide organisation that employs more than 100,000 co-workers in 44 countries. A key success factor is the recruitment of people

The president's message

At IKEA we often talk about taking 'many small steps forward'. This is the way IKEA has been built up over the years, and we adopt the same approach when it comes to social and environmental responsibility.

We know how difficult it is to change minds and break habits, but we believe that progress can be made and goals can be reached by moving forward step by step. Our ambition is to always strive forward and become better. This also applies to our co-operation with suppliers. All social and environmental activities help us and our suppliers produce more efficiently and profitably. Factories are run better and working conditions are improved, which benefits owners as well as employees. It is a win-win situation.

IKEA works towards sustainable business with complete commitment, as we believe in sourcing from emerging markets. To succeed, all parties involved should understand the challenges involved, and work jointly toward common goals. In my opinion, it is important that all stakeholders – IKEA, suppliers, governments, labour, and employer organisations – understand and share the same view. All of us must agree to long-term goals, such as meeting demands for working conditions and the environment. These goals have to be defined in legislation, global standards, and each company's code of conduct. Doing business in emerging economies is overwhelmingly positive; production costs are lower, our customers get better prices, and IKEA remains competitive. Moreover, it benefits communities and society at large.

We focus on two main types of activities. First, we work to follow the requirements in our code of conduct: 'The IKEA Way on Purchasing Home Furnishing Products' (IWAY). A significant aspect of this job is to make sure our suppliers and their sub-contractors fulfil the requirements of IWAY. Second, we work with projects and activities that respond to specific needs or situations. The IKEA Group works jointly with well-known and respected organisations, such as Save the Children, UNICEF, WWF, and others that offer expertise, experience and a presence in many areas throughout the world.

We have seen a very good rate of improvement over the past years. Suppliers are working continuously towards fulfilling our minimum requirements. Although we are pleased with the rate of development, a lot of work still remains to be done. It is a process that consists of many small steps, and with each one we learn, improve and raise our ambitions.

Source: Anders Dahlvig, President and CEO,
IKEA Group (IKEA, 2005, p. 7)

who share the IKEA vision and values and work together to realise those values. The IKEA human-resource policy is to provide co-workers with opportunities to grow as individuals and in their professional roles. In addition to the ability to do a good job, IKEA looks for personal qualities – such as a strong desire to learn and improve, common sense, ability to lead by example, efficiency, and humility.

IKEA encourages people to look for new and better ways of doing things in every aspect of their work. This helps IKEA to remain innovative, flexible, and responsive. IKEA thus offers co-workers opportunities and responsibility.

IKEA selects people who are strong leaders and who embrace the IKEA vision and culture. IKEA ensures that managers have appropriate training and ability to ensure the professional development of the co-workers in their teams. IKEA managers are expected to act as role models for their teams. IKEA supports managers by providing training that ensures a thorough understanding of the company's culture and values.

Products and material

When IKEA creates a new product, it considers the impact the product has on the environment and on the health of the user. All products must meet strict IKEA requirements for durability, design, use, safety, and care of the environment. To reduce the amount of resources that are used, renewable and recycled raw materials are used whenever possible. This not only enables IKEA to be more environmentally friendly, but also assists in keeping prices low for its customers.

IKEA encourages 'smart' solutions that minimise material use without adversely affecting the functionality or appearance of the product. Wood, metal, plastic, glass, bamboo, and textiles are the main raw materials used in IKEA products.

'Smart' packaging is another effective way in which IKEA is able to reduce an adverse impact on the environment. Product packaging and transportation are planned during the early stages of the design process.

Clever design and flat packaging help IKEA to fit more products into every load-carrying unit, whether this be by ship, truck, or train.

Supply chain

IKEA believes in safe, healthy, non-discriminatory working conditions and the protection of the environment throughout its supply chain. Remaining close to its suppliers is seen as the key to effective long-term co-operation. The company buys products from 1,300 suppliers in 53 countries. Co-workers in the trading-service offices monitor the production of IKEA products. This enables them to test new ideas, negotiate prices, and check quality while observing social and working conditions among suppliers.

IKEA introduced its own code of conduct ('IWAY') in 2000, and since then the firm has developed it further. IWAY defines what suppliers can expect from IKEA and what IKEA requires from its suppliers in terms of legal requirements, working conditions, the active prevention of child labour, care of the external environment, and forestry management.

The experience of Nicolae Borsos, an IKEA supplier in Romania, demonstrates the way in which the code of conduct operates. In 1999, with IKEA's help, Borsos bought a run-down furniture factory in the town of Nehoiu. Since then, an investment programme has increased profitability and improved conditions for the factory's 680 employees. All new investments were required to meet IKEA criteria for product quality, working conditions, and care of the external environment. In addition, Borsos was responsible for ensuring that his suppliers also respected the code of conduct. According to Borsos: 'The IWAY has resulted in a general improvement in standards in the factory' (Edvardsson *et al.*, 2006).

Sundström and Wilert (2005) have studied the implementation of the IWAY code of conduct in China. Their study demonstrated the difficulties that can arise when global firms attempt to implement universal codes in countries where local laws and customs can cause conflict. The first attempt to implement IWAY failed in its efforts to integrate the code of conduct into existing purchasing routines. Later attempts were more successful when IKEA started to work more directly with the supplier by using such initiatives as workshops and training sessions to help the suppliers to understand their crucial position in the IKEA supply chain from a CSR point of view.

IKEA believes in building long-term supplier relationships with suppliers who share its commitment to social work and environmental practices, and who want to grow and develop in partnership with IKEA.

Wood

IKEA recognises that the world's forests have essential functions in terms of water cycles, storing carbon, and supporting a large proportion of naturally occurring bio-diversity. IKEA thus ensures that it does not use wood from areas in the world where forests are being devastated. IKEA recognises forests as valuable resources, and the company therefore works to ensure that the wood used in IKEA products comes from well-managed forests that will continue to provide resources for future generations.

Wood is an excellent material for IKEA products from both a functional and an environmental perspective. Wood has the requisite properties to be the principal material in approximately 50 per cent of all IKEA products; in addition, the resource is renewable and recyclable. However, if wood is to remain a viable environmental choice, it must be sourced from responsibly managed forests. In this regard, IKEA has developed a four-step model to ensure that all wood used by the firm is sourced from certified forests.

To maintain low prices, IKEA must use its resources as effectively as possible. There are numerous examples of the cost consciousness of IKEA resulting in benefits for the environment. One example is the production of furniture from rubber-tree wood. The wood of these trees was previously classed as burnable waste after the supply of latex from the trees had dried up. This changed when IKEA decided to use these trees as furniture material instead. This kept production costs low and helped to reduce unnecessary waste.

Preventing child labour

IKEA has been working for many years to prevent child labour in India by fighting its root causes. The complexity of the issue of child labour requires input from many different parties if a sustainable solution is to be achieved. The following narrative provides insights into the multifaceted nature of this complex problem.

A collaborative venture between IKEA and a local company, Winrock International India, aims to provide solar lamps to people in approximately 200 villages without electricity in the Indian state of Pradesh. According to IKEA's Children's Ombudsman, Marianne Barner: 'Our cooperation with Winrock gives people access to good-quality lamps at a cheap price with a service guarantee. It's a way of providing help for self-help.' In villages with no electricity, solar lamps are a healthier and more environmentally friendly alternative than paraffin lamps or blazing fires. In addition, the lamps also provide indirect help in combating child labour. 'If children can do their homework in the evenings and maintain their interests in education, they'll be less inclined to start work at an early age,' observed Barner.

In addition, in August 2000, IKEA and UNICEF initiated a joint child-rights project in the same villages to establish so-called 'alternative learning centres' (ALCs). The project aims to mobilise these rural communities around strategies that are designed to prevent child labour. School enrolment drives are conducted to establish ALCs as a transition to formal primary schooling. Quality educational opportunities for children are essential to the prevention of child labour, and this IKEA initiative complements the government's efforts to enrol all children aged 6–12 years of age in primary school. As a result, more than 80 per cent of the 24,000 children who were previously out-of-school in these 200 villages were attending primary school in 2004. The remaining 20 per cent are covered by 99 ALCs, which are promoted as a 'bridging strategy' to coax children into mainstream education.

The solar lamps also enable village women in India's impoverished 'carpet belt' to earn much-needed extra income by sewing at home in the evenings. According to Barner: 'Their earnings are a valuable addition to a family's economy. This also reduces the pressure on the children to work.'

To show that IKEA was serious in its efforts to tackle the problem of child labour, Marianne Barner became IKEA's first children's ombudsman in 1998. Her role is to educate the organisation about the problem and to work actively towards a better life for the children affected by it. IKEA works in collaboration with UNICEF to tackle the roots of the problem – which include poverty, lack of education, and embedded cultural norms. The programme appears to have been successful, although it is difficult to obtain accurate measures of the effect of the work (Enquist *et al.,* 2007; Luce, 2004).

Environmental aspects of business

In addition to using resources wisely, IKEA strives to minimise adverse environmental effects caused by its business activities. In general terms, IKEA attempts to reduce carbon dioxide emissions, use alternative energy sources, manage waste, and decrease energy consumption. More specifically, methodical environmental work takes place at individual IKEA locations around the world. The focus is on the stores and distribution centres, where the majority of operations are conducted and where the majority of IKEA co-workers carry out their tasks. This is where the impact will be the greatest.

IKEA is not only working on environmental issues at IKEA locations. IKEA also has societal programmes at both the local level and the global level. For example, IKEA works actively in the United States in replanting trees and preserving the environment. In 2006, the company ran a campaign in which IKEA customers were asked to donate a dollar to plant a tree. IKEA then matched the donations for the first 100,000 trees planted.

IKEA and American Forests, a non-profit conservation organisation, then planted approximately 300,000 trees across the United States to help reduce carbon dioxide pollution and to renew America's forests. This initiative was recognised by the Natural Resources Council of America, which gave IKEA an award for the 'best environmental innovation in 2007'. As Deborah Gangloff, executive director of American Forests explained: 'This program is a testament to the commitment of IKEA to good environmental stewardship, and also to IKEA's customers for their concern for forests and ecosystems in North America'.

IKEA is also supporting a project entitled 'Sow a Seed in Borneo' in partnership with the Swedish University of Agricultural Sciences, the Yayasan Sabah Group, and the Malaysian forestry company RBJ. The project aims to re-forest and maintain 18,500 hectares of lowland rainforest in Sabah on the Malaysian island of Borneo. More than one million trees have been planted through this project, and IKEA has promised to protect the area from logging for the next 50 years. The project has also contributed to the building of homes, meeting places for social events, and field accommodation for more than 150 workers and their families who work with the project.

Community involvement and stakeholder cooperation

IKEA initiates and supports a wide range of stakeholder activities and projects globally and locally. In general terms, IKEA aims to improve health and education (focusing on children and women) and to protect the environment (focusing on forestry). In these projects, IKEA works in partnership with many companies, trade unions, and organisations throughout the world. These partnerships enable a sharing of experiences and ensure that the projects accomplish more than IKEA could have achieved by working alone on social and environmental issues.

The work against child labour (noted previously) also includes working with the Indian government to immunise all children against a range of infectious diseases. Disabilities and other medical problems cost money, and child labour is often a result of a lack of money in families. The immunisation programme diminishes the risk of disabilities and other health problems in children, thus decreasing the likelihood that families will be forced to send their children to work.

IKEA is also involved in a project to provide low-cost loans to women in the communities. This decreases their need to turn to 'loan sharks' in the area. The project pays a certain amount per month to self-help groups for impoverished women. This enables the women to open their own 'bank', from which they can borrow at a market price, rather than being forced to borrow from unscrupulous money-lenders at inflated prices. These loans enable the women to invest in such projects as a small store, an irrigation system, or other projects that can provide an income. This is especially important because many of these women's husbands have left the villages to find jobs in the cities, and not all of them are sending back money to their families.

Strategic perspective on values for a sustainable business

The environmental problems faced by IKEA over the years have been transformed in numerous small steps from a threat to the company's reputation (and possibly its existence) to an opportunity to use social and environmental issues in a proactive manner by virtue of the company's vision of everyday business contributing to genuine long-term sustainability. The norms and values of the service culture of IKEA have been, at one level, regulators of what is possible and not possible, and, on a higher level, have acted as a source of energy and direction for every co-worker and manager. In many ways, this is the essence of effective strategy-making. In a large and decentralised organisation that has operations in many countries, as is the case with IKEA, it is not possible for a strategy to lead to coordinated and effective activity unless the culture of the organisation provides the necessary energy and direction. The IKEA culture provides both *guidelines for action* and *meaning for what is done* at all levels of the organisation.

The values-based culture of IKEA thus facilitates work coordination, strategy implementation, quality control, and price control in a service-dominant logic that aims to create value for customers. The service culture is driven by the inner convictions of managers and co-workers alike, as well as being driven by external pressure from customers and competitors. Service leadership in these circumstances has to do with managing the dialectical relationship between culture and strategy.

IKEA can be understood as a *stakeholder network* of shared values and meanings. The interactions among the stakeholders are social constructs that produce (and reproduce) the IKEA service culture. In recounting the IKEA 'saga', the official narratives of the company reveal that the underlying basis of this construction (and reconstruction) of service culture is the continuous regeneration of values and meanings at all levels of the IKEA network.

The saga of IKEA can also be viewed from an environmental perspective. As a 'globally integrated enterprise', IKEA is a complex network with a multicultural character. But the essential 'virtues' of IKEA are rooted in the heritage of the rural Swedish region in which the company was born; moreover, they are embedded in the history of the company. These enduring essential values are discernible despite the variety of cultural expressions in which the company functions – whether this is in the USA, Germany, China, Sweden, or elsewhere. In short, the service culture of IKEA is a distinctive set of values and meanings for sustainable business, deeply embedded in the history of the firm.

Questions

1   How can social and environmental values be a driving force in a company to develop beyond 'commoditisation'?
2   How do the narratives that are embedded in the corporate history of your company affect the current business culture?
3   How does service culture drive service strategy?
4   What do social and environmental values mean for creating customer value?
5   What impact does a 'code of conduct' have on the supplier chain?
6   Is social and environmental responsibility only for big firms?
7   How can your organisation build a culture of 'sustainable business'?

References

Edvardsson, B. and Enquist, B. (2002) 'The IKEA Saga': how service culture drives service strategy, *The Service Industries Journal*, Vol. 22, No. 4, pp. 153–86.
Edvardsson, B., Enquist, B. and Hay, M. (2006) Values based service brands: narratives from IKEA, *Managing Service Quality*, Vol. 16, No. 3, pp. 230–46.
Elkington, J. (1997) *Cannibals with Forks – The Triple Bottom Line of the 21st Century Business.* Oxford: Capstone Publishing.
Enquist, B., Edvardsson, B. and Petros Sebhatu, S. (2007) Values based service quality for sustainable business, *Managing Service Quality*, Vol. 17, No. 4, pp. 385–403.
Friedman, T.L. (2005) *The World is Flat: A Brief History of the Globalized World in the Twenty-first Century.* London: Penguin Books.
Konzelmann, S.J., Wilkinson, F., Craypo, C. and Aridi, R. (2005) *The Export of National Varieties of Capitalism: The Cases of Wallmart and IKEA.* Centre for Business Research, University of Cambridge Working Paper, No. 314.
IKEA (2003) The Natural Step Organizational Case Summary. IKEA.
IKEA (2005) *IKEA Social and Environmental Responsibility Report.* Corporate PR, IKEA Services AB.
IKEA (2006a) *IKEA Social and Environmental Responsibility Report.* Corporate PR, IKEA Services AB.
IKEA (2006b) IKEA and American Forests Receive Natural Resources Council of America Award for Landmark Environmental Program, Press release, Dec. 6.
IKEA (2006c) Patterns for Progress, Green Bean Production, DVD from Inter IKEA Systems BV.

Luce, E. (2004) Ikea's grown up plan to tackle child labour, *Financial Times*, September 15.

Morgan, A. (2004) *The Pirate Inside. Building a Challenger Brand Culture within Yourself and Your Organization*. Chichester: John Wiley & Sons.

Palmisano, S.J. (2006) The globally integrated enterprise, *Foreign Affairs*, Vol. 85, No.3, May/June.

Papanek, V. (1995) IKEA and the future: a personal view. *Democratic Design from IKEA of Sweden because of 50 Years Anniversary of IKEA*, published by IKEA of Sweden.

Salzer, M. (1994) *Identity Across Borders: A Study in the 'IKEA-World'*. Linköping: Department of Management & Economics, Linköping University. Diss.

Sundström, M. and Wilert, M. (2005) Global codes, local rules implementing codes of conduct in China – the case of IWAY. Master's thesis, Institute of International Business, Stockholm School of Economics.

Torekull, B. (1998) *Historian om IKEA*. Stockholm: Wahlström & Widstrand

Torekull, B. (1999) *Leading by Design: The IKEA Story*. New York: Harper Business.

Waddock, S. and Bodwell, C. (2007) *Total Responsibility Management: The Manual*. Sheffield: Greenleaf Publishing.

3 Values-based service

Introduction

This chapter discusses the conceptual basis of a values-based, sustainable, and profitable service business.

According to Ramirez (1999), the notion of 'value' has been a subject of interest since the time of the ancient Greeks; moreover, the concept of 'value' (in both the moral sense and the economic sense) was studied under the umbrella of moral philosophy until the eighteenth century, when economics became a field of study in its own right. Since then, the economic and ethical aspects of the concept of 'value' have been separated. On the economic side, value is about *utility*, whereas, on the ethical side, it is about *judgement*.

Gustafsson and Johnson (2003) analyzed how to compete in a service economy and emphasize the key role the customers have in value co-creation. The companies must involve customers in service development in new ways and early in development projects.

Normann and Ramirez (1998, p. 69) suggested that 'the key to creating value is to co-produce offerings that mobilize customers'. According to this view, much of customer value is the outcome of service experiences (Carbone, 2004; Meyer and Schwager, 2007), and a company should therefore orchestrate customer experiences that render value whenever customers interact with the firm and its products and services. This view of value emphasises the importance of the customers' activities, involvement, emotions, and experiences in assessing value-in-use. This emphasis on the activities of customers means that companies can only make *value propositions*, which have the objective of supporting the customers in their own value-creating activities. Such a customer value proposition is therefore defined from the *customer's* perspective and promises the customer *value-in-use*. In this regard, Grönroos (2000, pp. 24–5) emphasised the importance of *time* and *relationship* in creating value:

Value for customers is created throughout the relationship by the customer ... in interactions between the customer and the supplier or service provider. The focus is not on products but on the customers' value-creating processes where value emerges for customers and is perceived by them.

Against this background, it is apparent that the logic of value creation is changing. The traditional view was that value is defined and created in the value chain – that is, upstream suppliers provide input, the focal company adds value, and the product is then passed on downstream. According to this view, value is *embedded* in products or service offerings, and companies should therefore position themselves in a value chain. The emerging view differs from this traditional understanding by conceiving value as something that is *co-created with customers*, and then assessed by them on the basis of value-in-use and consumption experiences. According to this emerging view, the customer defines value and the assessment of value is linked to the customer's needs, wants, values, knowledge, and skills, but also resonance.

In summary, the traditional view of value is *attribute-based* and *offering-related*, whereas the emerging view is *customer-based* and *use-related*.

Customer co-created value

When a service becomes real in action, value-in-use is realised for the customer (Vargo and Lusch, 2004; Edvardsson *et al.*, 2005). A service business that is based on the paradigm of 'service-dominant logic' (SDL) is essentially customer-oriented and relational (Vargo and Lusch, 2004, 2008). According to this paradigm, service is defined as the application of specialised competences (operant resources of knowledge and skill) doing something beneficial for, and in conjunction with, an entity as part of an exchange process (Vargo and Lusch, 2008). SDL is thus resource-centred. Operant resources can act on (or in concert with) other resources to provide benefit and create value. This represents a major conceptual shift – from an emphasis on output to an emphasis on mutually satisfying interactive processes. It also represents a shift from static resources (such as plant and equipment) to dynamic resources (such as employees, competences, value-creation partners, and customers). In the ultimate scenario, SDL envisages the co-creation of value through resource integration (Vargo and Lusch, 2008).

The concept of customer value

Although Vargo and Lusch (2004, 2008) introduced SDL as a new logic for marketing, Holbrook (2006) contended that his 'concept of customer value' (CCV), which was introduced twenty years before SDL, is also about business as a value-creating endeavour.

Four pillars of customer value

According to Holbrook (2006), customer value rests on four pillars.

First, customer value is *interactive in* that it involves a relationship between the customer and goods or services. No value exists without this interaction.

Second, customer value *is relativistic. In* this regard, value is: (i) comparative (depending on the relative merits of one object compared with another); (ii) situational (varying from one evaluative context to another); and (iii) personal (differing from one individual to the next).

Third, value refers to *a judgement of performance or outcome.* In this regard, value can be expressed in terms of: (i) attitude (like/dislike); (ii) affect (favourable/unfavourable); (iii) valence (positive/negative); (iv) evaluation (good/bad); (v) opinion (positive/negative); (vi) satisfaction (high/low); (vii) behavioural tendency (approach/avid); and/or (viii) choice (choose/reject).

Fourth, customer value resides in *a consumption or use experience* (rather than in a physical product or service).

On the basis of these four pillars, Holbrook (2006), developed a typology of customer value (as shown in Table 3.1).

As shown in the table, the typology is based on three dimensions ('extrinsic/intrinsic'; 'self-oriented/other-oriented'; and 'active/reactive'). These three dimensions result in eight categories of customer value. With

Table 3.1   Typology of customer value

		Extrinsic	Intrinsic
Self-oriented	*Active*	EFFICIENCY	PLAY
	Reactive	EXCELLENCE (quality)	AESTHETICS (beauty)
Other-oriented	*Active*	STATUS (fashion)	ETHICS (justice, virtue, morality)
	Reactive	ESTEEM (materialism)	SPIRITUALITY (rapture, ecstasy)

Source: Holbrook (2006, p

regard to the first dimension ('extrinsic/intrinsic'), Holbrook (2006, p. 213) explained:

> Value is *extrinsic* when some object or experience serves as the means to an end, performing a function that is instrumental in nature. By contrast, *intrinsic* value refers to the case in which an experience is prized for its own sake – that is, self-justified as an autotelic end in itself.

The qualities of efficiency and excellence are two examples of attributes within the extrinsic dimension, whereas aesthetics (beauty) and ethics (justice, virtue, morality) lie within the intrinsic dimension.

Holbrook (2006) conceptualised value at the level of the individual customer. He included the notion of 'values' (in the sense of 'ideals') within the intrinsic dimension of customer value (ethics), but he did not pay explicit attention to 'values' in the extrinsic dimension. It is the contention of the present book that CSR (that is, extrinsic social and environmental responsibility) is inescapably intertwined with the corporate values of the providers of market offerings. At the company level, three categories of such values can be discerned: ethical, social, and environmental. These values guide customers in their assessments of value-in-use, and they also guide companies in formulating their value propositions in the first place.

Customer value and value propositions

The logic of value creation and the logic of values, taken together, thus constitute the theoretical frame of reference for all value propositions. As already noted in this book, the cultural expression and value propositions of IKEA are essentially about *shared values* and *shared meanings*. Indeed, according to Salzer (1994), the 'success story' of IKEA is essentially based on producing (and co-producing) such collective meanings.

Rintamäki *et al.* (2007) suggested four situations in which the key dimensions of customer value as the basis for value propositions will differ. First, if *economic value* is the key motivator for the customers, the value proposition should focus on price. Second, if *functional value* is the key motivator, the value proposition should focus on solutions. Third if *emotional value* is the key motivator for the customers, the focus should be on customer experiences. Fourth, if *symbolic value* is the key motivator, the value proposition should focus on meaning.

The logic of value and the logic of values

The logic of value and the logic of values can be summarised as shown in Table 3.2. The logic of value emphasises business models that have a financial and commercial focus, whereas the logic of values emphasises the social and environmental dimensions (Edvardsson and Enquist, 2002; Edvardsson *et al.*, 2006).

In a values-based service company, the business model is grounded in the paradigm of SDL, which, in turn, is based on the core company values, the foundation values (social and environmental responsibility), and the customers' values. Moreover, the logic of values drives the business strategy, which is expressed in the design of a business model, the definition of the business goals, and the choice of performance indicators.

The logic of value is combined with the logic of values in forming the basis of the IKEA culture (and thus forming the basis for a values-based, sustainable, and profitable service business). Examples of this combination of logics can be found in a booklet entitled 'The Key' (IKEA, 1995). This booklet describes a cornerstone of the IKEA culture – the wise use of resources while minimising waste:

> It's all about understanding how, by continuing to make the most rational use of energy and materials, we can reduce our costs and do the planet a favour at the same time … The [IKEA] range and our purchasing operations are the basis for our success. This is where everything begins. If things go wrong here, [they will] go wrong all along the line: from our choice of material via manufacturing techniques, through the labyrinth of logistics and distribution, all the way to the store, where our customers would just stand shaking their heads at the price tag. We have often said that we are one of the world's very few retailers who are steered by production … It is the key to our success … The biggest secret is the advantage we have at the production stage. This creates the conditions for the vital third dimension – a low price.

Table 3.2   The logic of value and the logic of values

The logic of value	The logic of values
Extrinsic	Intrinsic
Short-term financial calculations	Social and environmental calculations
Control-based business model	Values-based business model
Quality, time, and price	Shared values and meanings

'The Key' contains many examples of how IKEA combined functionality with high quality and a low price. The booklet also discusses the importance of the environmental values of the company:

> The longest relationship of all is the one that humankind has with the environment that has fostered its progress. If we are to preserve that precious environment, we must use raw materials in the most rational way possible, never letting anything go to waste. This is something that suits IKEA ... The environmentalists' call to use natural resources sparingly could have been formulated by anyone who is a true 'IKEAn'. After all, the concept of 'waste not, want not' has been dear to our hearts for years.

These quotations from 'The Key' reveal that IKEA is driven by a combination of economic values (cost efficiency) and environmental values (no waste).

This 'logic of values' within a company must coincide with the values of customers. If a company is associated with practices that are perceived to be unethical, customers are likely to avoid such providers. Companies that emphasise social and environmental responsibility thus add value-in-use for customers, whereas companies that violate commonly held norms and values that are important to customers and other stakeholders will destroy value and endanger their sustainable success.

The history of IKEA demonstrates that a culture that is based on a logic of values that makes sense *inside* the company, as well as for customers and other stakeholders *outside* the company, is a strong driving force in business development. In combination with a focused understanding of the economic realities of value-creation logic (attractive product attributes, time, and cost), 'attractive values' add to customer value-in-use.

CSR and the business case of sustainability

Corporate social responsibility (CSR) has become a driving force in many service businesses. An ethical company with a strong sense of social and environmental responsibility addresses the concerns of its main stakeholders – including its customers, employees, the media, suppliers, shareholders, and investors (Waddock, 2006).

CSR is, to some extent, a new management challenge. However, the topic of social responsibility has been discussed in general terms in the management and marketing literature for decades (Berle and Means, 1932). Indeed, Lazer (1969, p. 3) called for a broader understanding of the marketing concept 40 years ago when he argued for marketing to extend beyond the short-term profit focus to become 'an institution of social control instrumental in reorienting a culture from a producer's to a consumer's culture'.

The contemporary understanding of CSR refers to a company's commitment to its social and environmental obligations in forming 'bonds' with customers and other stakeholders. Values linked to CSR have become incorporated into the core values of many companies, and it has become increasingly apparent that a company that does not meet the requirements of customers in terms of ethical, environmental, and social values will suffer so-called 'value dissonance' and attract negative media publicity that will drive customers away.

It is thus apparent that CSR is an important concept for any company that wishes to secure a sustainable future as a going concern with growth and profitability. This thinking is an integral aspect of IKEA's business model and organisational culture.

The need for such enhanced awareness and utilisation of CSR in service businesses has been brought into focus by recent criticisms of prevailing marketing practices. For example, Gummesson (2006) has criticised an exaggerated and simplistic reliance on the marketing concept of customer needs and satisfaction, which seems to have become something of a 'highway to profit'. According to this view, maximisation of short-term profit has become the only purpose of business, with corporate citizenship being diluted to the status of 'charity' and an apparent blindness to the effects of unethical activity and 'black economies'.

Nevertheless, the appropriate role of CSR in business management has long been a subject of debate. Friedman (1970) questioned whether a business can have any 'responsibilities' other than the responsibility to increase its profits; however, other authors have disagreed. Grant (1991) dismissed Friedman's restricted point of view as fallacious. Carroll (1991) argued for a 'pyramid' of four kinds of social responsibilities – economic, legal, ethical, and philanthropic – thus integrating CSR with a stakeholder perspective. The changing nature of CSR has also been debated. Andriof *et al.* (2002) argued that the prevailing business imperatives in CSR were originally 'profitability', 'compliance', and 'philanthropy'; however, these authors asserted that, from the end of the 1970s and onwards, the prevailing business imperative became 'corporate social responsiveness'. Zadek (2001) has also referred to the idea of 'responsiveness' in calling for 'responsible corporate citizenship'. In a similar vein, Elkington (2001) has argued that '... citizen CEOs and corporations can fuse values and value creation'.

Vogel (2005a, 2005b) utilised a broader concept of CSR when describing it as 'the market for virtue'. In discussing whether there is a business case for CSR, Vogel (2005a, 2005b) noted that CSR does make business sense for some firms in specific circumstances. Xueming and Bhattacharya (2006) showed that there is a positive relationship between CSR and profit in the case of *innovative* firms, but that the opposite applies in less innovative firms. Roberts (2001) argued that CSR provides a new form of 'visibility' (that is, environmental, social, and ethical 'visibility') as a supplement to financial visibility. In his view, CSR does not represent a genuine commitment to ethics; rather, he characterised CSR as the 'ethics of Narcissus' – that is, not so much a real concern for others as a preoccupation with being *seen* to be concerned for others.

Contrary to Roberts (2001), the present book contends that a business case can be made in which CSR is an important prerequisite for a sustainable business. The most commonly accepted definition of sustainability was provided in the report entitled *Our Common Future*, which was produced by the United Nations. According to this definition (Brundtland, 1987, p. 43), sustainable development is '... development that meets the needs of the present without compromising the ability of future generations to meet their own needs'. Drawing on this understanding of sustainability, a 'sustainable business' is understood in this book as *a long-term successful business built on co-created competitive customer value combined with ethical, social, and environmental responsibility.*

This definition of a sustainable business utilises the 'triple bottom line' (TBL) (Elkington, 1997) noted previously – that is, a bottom line that takes account of economic, social, and environmental perspectives. TBL emphasises the importance of equilibrium among three basic interests that are often considered to be in conflict: economic prosperity, environmental regeneration, and social equity (Elkington, 1997, 2001). According to Elkington (1997), a business is sustainable when it reaches long-term financial stability by minimising its environmental impact and acting in conjunction with the community's social and cultural expectations.

IKEA represents an outstanding example of a 'sustainable business' conceived in these terms. As the president and CEO of IKEA, Anders Dahlvig, observed (IKEA, 2006. p. 7):

> I have always been of the opinion that an inclusive approach to social and environmental responsibility makes good business sense. Not only does it create positive feelings amongst our customers and co-workers, it also has a positive impact on our business. And, in many cases it has also proven to be cost-efficient.

CSR and competitive advantage

Gummesson (2006) was critical of mainstream marketing in which corporate citizenship (which can be seen as part of CSR) is diluted into mere charity. However, as Vogel (2005a) has noted, such an understanding of corporate citizenship (as 'charity') represents the old style of CSR, and Andriof *et al.* (2002) have confirmed this shift in understanding. According to Vogel (2005b), the emerging understanding of CSR has shifted from 'doing good to do good' to 'doing good to do well'.

In a similar vein, Porter and Kramer (2002) have shown that charitable philanthropy is in decline but, when used in a proactive way, doing good can be a competitive advantage. As Porter and Kramer (2002, p. 57) observed: 'Most companies feel compelled to give to charity. Few have figured out how to do it well.' According to these authors, there has to be a convergence of interests between philanthropy and business. Such a convergence is seen to occur when corporate expenditure simultaneously produces social and economic gains.

CSR as part of an overall strategy

A values-based company such as IKEA uses CSR as part of its overall strategy of interaction with its stakeholders to co-create customer and stakeholder value (Enquist *et al.*, 2006). However, for this to work effectively, the values of CSR and the core corporate values of the firm have to complement one another.

CSR is not a new business concept, but it has recently achieved greater significance in the contemporary competitive globalised economy. The incorporation of CSR into a company's business strategy facilitates the creation of favourable bonds with customers and other stakeholders (such as employees and shareholders). The new understanding of CSR is, as Vogel (2005b) noted, about 'doing good to do well'.

Questions

1 How is the concept of customer value defined and used in your organisation?
2 What core company values contribute the most to customer value-in-use?
3 How can successful constellations of intrinsic and extrinsic value be managed?
4 How can CSR contribute to creating customer value?

5 How is the business case of sustainability used to create a sustainable business in your organisation?
6 Which values are most important for customers and other stakeholders?
7 Which values destroy customer value (and why)?

References

Anderson, J.C., Narus, J.A and Van Rossum, W. (2006) Customer value propositions in business markets, *Harvard Business Review*, Vol. 84, No. 3, pp. 91–9.
Andriof, J., Waddock, S., Husted, B. and Sutherland Rahman, S. (eds) (2002) *Unfolding Stakeholder Thinking: Theory, Responsibility and Engagement.* Sheffield: Greenleaf Publishing.
Berle, A. and Means, G.C. (1932) *The Modern Corporation and Private Property.* New York: Macmillan.
Brundtland, G.H. (1987) *Our Common Future: The World Commission on Environment and Development.* Oxford: Oxford University Press.
Carbone, L.P. (2004) *Clued In: How to Keep Customers Coming Back Again and Again.* Upper Saddle River, NJ: Prentice-Hall.
Carroll, A.B. (1991) The pyramid of corporate social responsibility: toward the moral management of organizational stakeholders, *Business Horizons*, July–August, pp. 39–48.
Edvardsson, B. and Enquist, B. (2002) The IKEA saga – how service culture drives service strategy, *The Service Industries Journal*, Vol. 22, No. 4, pp. 153–86.
Edvardsson, B., Enquist, B. and Hay, M. (2006) Values-based service brands: narratives from IKEA, *Managing Service Quality*, Vol. 16, No. 3, pp. 230–46.
Edvardsson, B., Enquist, B. and Johnston, B. (2005) Co-creating customer value through hyperreality in the pre-purchase service experience, *Journal of Service Research*, Vol. 8, No. 2, pp. 149–61.
Elkington, J. (1997) *Cannibals with Forks – The Triple Bottom Line of the 21st Century Business.* Oxford: Capstone Publishing.
Elkington, J. (2001) *The Chrysalis Economy: How Citizen CEOs and Corporation can Fuse Values and Value Creation.* Oxford: Capstone Publishing.
Enquist, B., Johnsson, M. and Skålén, P. (2006) Adoption of corporate social responsibility – incorporating a stakeholder perspective, *Qualitative Research in Accounting & Management*, Vol. 3, No. 3, pp. 188–207.
Friedman, M. (1970) The social responsibility of business is to increase its profit, *New York Times Magazine*, September 13.
Grant, C. (1991) Friedman fallacies, *Journal of Business Ethics*, Vol. 10, No. 12, pp. 907–14.
Grönroos, C. (2000) *Service Management and Marketing – A Customer Relationship Management Approach*, 2nd edition. Chichester: Wiley.
Gummesson, E. (2006) 'Many-to-many marketing as grand theory: a Nordic School contribution' in Lusch, R. F. and Vargo, S. L. (eds) *The Service-Dominant Logic of Marketing*, New York: M.E. Sharpe.

Gustafsson, A. and Johnson, M. D. (2003) *Competing in a Service Economy*. San Fransisco, CA: Jossey -Bass.

Hirshman, E.C. and Holbrook, M.B. (1982) Hedonic Consumption: emerging concepts, methods and propositions, *Journal of Marketing*, Vol. 46, Summer, pp. 92–101.

Holbrook, M.B. (2006) ROSEPEKICECIVEC versus CCV, in Lusch, R.F. and Vargo, S.L. (eds) *The Service-Dominant Logic of Marketing*, New York: M.E. Sharpe.

IKEA (1995) The Key, Inter IKEA Systems.

IKEA (2006) IKEA Social and Environmental Responsibility report. Corporate PR, IKEA Services AB.

Laczniak, G.R. (2006) Some societal and ethical dimensions of the service-dominant logic perspective of marketing, in Lusch, R.F. and Vargo, S.L. (eds) *The Service-Dominant Logic of Marketing*, New York: M.E. Sharpe.

Lazer, W. (1969) Marketing's changing social relationships, *Journal of Marketing*, Vol. 34, No. 1, pp. 3–9.

Lusch, R.F. and Vargo. S.I . (eds) (2006) *The Service-Dominant Logic of Marketing*. New York: M.E. Sharpe.

Meyer, C. and Schwager, A. (2007) Understanding customer experience, *Harvard Business Review*, Vol. 85, No. 2, pp. 116–26.

Normann, R. and Ramirez, R. (1998) *Designing Interactive Strategy from Value Chain to Value Constellation*, 2nd edition. Chichester: John Wiley and Sons.

Porter, M.E. and Kramer, M.R. (2002) The competitive advantage of corporate philanthropy, *Harvard Business Review*, December.

Ramirez, R. (1999) Value co-production: intellectual origins and implications for practice and research, *Strategic Management Journal*, Vol. 20, pp. 49–65.

Rintamäki, T., Kuusela, H. and Mitronen, L. (2007) Identifying competitive customer value propositions in retailing, *Managing Service Quality*, Vol. 17, No. 6, pp. 621–34.

Roberts, J. (2001) Corporate governance and the ethics of Narcissus, *Business Ethics Quarterly*, Vol. 11, No. 1, pp. 109–27.

Salzer, M. (1994) *Identity Across Borders: A Study in the 'IKEA-World'*. Linköping: Department of Management & Economics, Linköping University.

Steger, U. (ed.) (2004) *The Business of Sustainability: Building industry cases for corporate sustainability*, New York: Palgrave.

Vargo, S.L. and Lusch, R.F. (2004) Evolving to a new dominant logic of marketing, *Journal of Marketing*, Vol. 68, January, pp. 1–17.

Vargo, S.L. and Lusch, R.F. (2008) Service-dominant logic: continuing the evolution, *Journal of the Academy of Marketing Science* (online version).

Vogel, D. (2005a) *The Market for Virtue: The Potential and Limits of Corporate Social Responsibility*. Washington, DC: Brooking Institution Press.

Vogel, D. (2005b) The market for virtue? The business case for corporate social responsibility, *California Management Review*, Vol. 47, No. 4.

Waddock, S. (2006) *Leading Corporate Citizens: Vision, Values, Value Added*. New York: McGraw-Hill Higher Education.

Weick, K. E. (1995) *Sensemaking in Organizations.* Thousands Oaks, CA: Sage Publications.

Xueming, L. and Bhattacharya, C.B. (2006) Corporate social responsibility, customer satisfaction, and market value, *Journal of Marketing*, Vol. 70, October, pp. 1–18.

Zadek, S. (2001) *The Civil Corporation: The New Economy of Corporate Citizenship.* London: Earthscan and New Economics Foundation.

4 Values-based service experience

Introduction

When customers buy a product, such as a new car, they are allowed to test-drive the vehicle to experience its performance and handling. However, when customers wish to purchase a service – such as a tourist service, a home solution, a business solution, a medical service, or education – it can be difficult to provide customers with a 'test drive'. When test-driving a car, potential purchasers take the real car, in real time, down real streets, facing real situations. However, if a potential buyer were to test out a tourist service at a real resort, with real food, and real service, he or she would be experiencing the actual service. Nevertheless, in some service situations, service organisations can (and do) provide 'test drives'. Such experiences might involve a simulated activity in a simulated setting, thus enabling customers to assess value-in-use. This simulated reality, referred to as 'hyperreality', can take place in a so-called 'experience room'.

This chapter describes how a service provider can create such an 'experience room' to enable customers to test a service before it is purchased and consumed. The focus of the chapter is not on the nature of the service *per se*, but on the design of the experience room in which it is to be tested. The chapter, which is based on an article by Edvardsson *et al.* (2005, 2007), presents a new framework for designing such an experience room.

The experience room must express the core values that underlie the service experience and form the basis for the *values-based service* that is the focus of this book. These values include both the company's own core corporate values and the wider ethical, social, and environmental values of society at large.

The chapter introduces the concept of the 'experience room' with examples from IKEA, which aims to provide solutions to 'real-life problems at home'. The chapter discusses the benefits that can accrue to service providers as a result of creating such experience rooms, and suggests five dimensions to be considered in designing such an experience room.

Value creation through hyperreality and hyperreal services

To attract and keep customers, and thus make a profit, companies are always searching for new and better ways to create value and differentiate their market offerings (Shaw and Ivens, 2002; Bendapudi and Leone, 2003). In this regard, many organisations are increasingly focusing on *experiences* to engage customers and differentiate themselves (Voss 2003). According to Johnston and Clark (2001), excellent companies are often distinguished from average companies by these experiences, rather than by a logical cognitive assessment of value for money.

Personal values are often linked to the emotional responses of customers in these experiences. The objective functional qualities of the service are, in themselves, insufficient to provide a favourable experience – because an emotional reaction forms part of every customer's perception of a favourable quality experience (Cronin, 2003; Sherry, 1998; Mano and Oliver, 1993). 'Value-in-use' and 'consumption judgements' are related concepts. In both cases, the traditional focus on cognitive evaluations has been extended to include service-elicited emotions and experiences, which include the influence of values and a sense of social and environmental responsibility.

Prahalad and Ramaswamy (2004, p. 137), who focused on the co-creation of unique value with customers, argued that 'value is now centred in the experiences of consumers', rather than being embedded in products and services. Similarly, Berry *et al.* (2002) emphasised the importance of 'managing the total customer experience' in arguing that organisations should recognise clues about experiences related to functionality *and* clues about experiences related to emotions.

Providing customers with pre-purchase service experiences

Service providers are increasingly recognising the value that can be created by providing unique or memorable customer experiences. By extending such service experiences into the pre-purchase period, Edvardsson *et al.* (2005) contended that companies can:

- add unique and personalised value to the service;
- connect with the customer through exposure to the company's values;
- learn more about the customers' needs, desires, and values (and use this information to facilitate service development and quality improvement);
- increase loyalty;
- create a unique, values-based identity;

- manage customer expectations and quality-in-use; and
- improve sales.

In product-based organisations, customers can be involved in a pre-purchase experience. They can, for example, be closely involved in the design of a product. Prahalad and Ramaswamy (2004) cited the example of transforming the traditional process of buying a houseboat into an *individualised co-creation experience* by involving customers in the design process of the houseboat to be purchased. This is more difficult to achieve with services, but customers can, for example, discuss the nature of a surgical procedure with a doctor before the service is actually rendered.

Despite the difficulties of 'pre-experience testing' with services, it is the contention of this book that customers can be involved in testing a service to a much greater extent than has previously been the case (as, for example, simply discussing potential surgery with a doctor). By providing distinctive and memorable pre-purchase experiences in carefully designed experience rooms, organisations can dramatically transform the nature of their service offerings and manage customers' experiences in a more systematic way.

Experience room and hyperreal services

The notion of 'hyperreality' is linked to mental and symbolic processes (Normann, 2001). People frequently experience such 'hyperreality' in their everyday lives as they perceive representations of roles, relationships, values, and characteristics simulated on a cinema screen or television. These experiences are designed to provide consumers with the vicarious experience of another place, time, or reality.

According to Johnston and Clark (2001), a 'service experience' is a service process that creates customer responses (cognitive, emotional, and behavioural) that results in a mental 'mark' (or memory). The customers' values are part of their cognitive, emotional, and behavioural responses; depending on circumstances, the result can be either 'values dissonance' (causing an unfavourable service experience) or 'values resonance' (supporting a favourable service experience). A 'values-based service experience' thus refers to a service experience that the customer associates with attractive values, rather than merely associating the service with considerations of price-related functional qualities only.

The role of an 'experience room' is to help customers to assess the quality and value of a service and the service provider in context. Traditionally, customers have experienced services only during and after consumption. In contrast, an experience room enables customers to experience (and assess) the service *before* purchase and consumption. This is achieved by placing customers in a realistic situation that enables them to assess the service and the values it communicates.

Bitner (1992) coined the term 'servicescape' to denote the environment in which a service is realised and an experience created. Bitner (1992) suggested that the servicescape has three dimensions: (i) *ambient conditions* (such as temperature, air quality, and noise); (ii) *space/function* (such as layout, equipment, and furnishings); and (iii) *signs, symbols, and artefacts* (such as signage, décor, and personal artefacts). The notion of the 'servicescape' thus tends to emphasise physical artefacts. Environmental factors (ambient conditions, space and function, and signs and symbols) drive internal responses (cognitive, emotional, and physiological) that affect behaviour in terms of 'approach' (affiliation, exploration, staying longer, and so on), 'avoidance' (opposite of approach), and 'social interactions' (between and among customers and employees).

This book argues that a comprehensive description and analysis of customer experiences requires attention to both the mental *and* the physical aspects of the experience. The experience room is a place for creating customer value in the pre-purchase phase by enabling the customer to 'taste' and assess the real value of a service experience prior to purchase and consumption.

Design dimensions of the experience room

Five dimensions underpin the design of experience rooms: (i) physical artefacts; (ii) intangible artefacts; (iii) technology; (iv) customer placement; and (v) customer involvement. All of these contribute to the creation of a 'hyperreal' service experience.

Physical artefacts

Physical artefacts include physical signs and symbols, products, and the infrastructure required to create the physical attributes of the experience room (Bitner, 1992; Normann, 2001; Venkatesh, 1999). Some of the physical artefacts have a direct impact on the co-created service experience, whereas others exert only an indirect influence. Buildings, equipment, and physical products are used by customers to make inferences regarding the nature of an intangible service.

Intangible atrefacts

Intangible artefacts can include mental images, brand reputation, and themes (Bitner, 1992). Such intangible elements, which are used to promote a favourable customer experience, often represent company culture and strategy. They help people to envisage how the service can create a positive experience of value.

Experiences based upon themes engendered by pictures, films, music, and activities stimulate customer imaging (Arnould *et al.*, 1998). Intangible artefacts also communicate the norms and values of the company, which enhances the likelihood of achieving 'resonance' with the values of the individual customer.

Technology

In its broadest sense, technology enhances 'hyperreality' through simulations of how activities and service processes are carried out. The aim is to 'touch' the customer and infer quality through meaning, arousal, and excitement. In this regard, Venkatesh (1999, p. 155) has observed: 'With the emergence of new technologies of information and communication, the visual is supplanting the textual as the cultural order'.

Technology must be considered as a distinctive dimension of the 'experience room' because it can create memorable sensations that have a profound impact on the overall experience of the customer. In addition, technology (especially self-service technology) can actually change the role of the customer with regard to the co-production and co-creation of experiences (Prahalad and Ramaswamy, 2004).

Customer placement

An experience room focuses on the placement of customers, rather than the placement of products (as in a showroom). Customer placement determines the nature of interactions with other persons (and with products) in a defined 'hyperreal' environment.

All customer experiences are unique and personal. The drivers of these experiences can be extrinsic or intrinsic. *Extrinsic* drivers are registered and interpreted within the customer's own cognitive and emotional framework. *Intrinsic* drivers include the customer's personal values and the meanings that each customer attaches to those values. Social and environmental values are more important for some customers than for others.

Customer involvement

According to Swaminathan *et al.* (1996, p. 52), customer involvement consists of:

… the conscious, bridging experiences, connections or references … that the viewer makes between his own life and [a] stimulus … Involvement results from an interaction between person, stimulus, and situation.

A distinction can be made between *cognitive* involvement and *affective* involvement in consumption situations (Park and Young, 1984). Through a combination of the two, individuals in the experience room become involved and active in co-creating favourable experiences in accordance with individualised 'scripts' (Normann, 2001; Prahalad and Ramaswamy, 2004).

The 'hyperreal' service experience

The 'hyperreal' service experience is the result of interpreting the physical artefacts, intangible artefacts, technology, and events that occur in the experience room. To some extent, the experience can be controlled by the provider, but the customer is mainly in control. Even if several customers are all in the same experience room, the service experience will vary from customer to customer – because these people have different needs and memories, as well as applying different values when assessing a service process and outcome.

The service experience is affected by the customer's perceptions of the various dimensions of the 'hyperreal' service in the experience room. If the experience is positive, the desired outcome is the purchase and the consumption of the 'real' service. The dimensions of the experience room are presented in Figure 4.1.

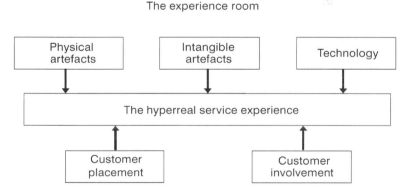

Figure 4.1 The design dimensions of the experience room (This figure first appeared in *Journal of Service Research*, Vol. 8, No. 2 (2005), pp. 149–61. With permission from Sage Publications)

It is important to emphasise the role of the customer in co-creating the experience in the 'hyperreal' environment. The provider must involve and 'touch' the consumer by creating meaning, pleasure, and excitement through physical artefacts, intangible artefacts, customer placement, customer involvement, and technology. The aim is to co-create attractive (but realistic) values-based experiences. Table 4.1 provides a summary of the five design dimensions of an experience room and a brief description of each.

Illustrations of values-based service experience from IKEA

IKEA experience rooms

In general, IKEA 'experience rooms' around the world are designed in much the same way and most of the furniture comes from the same collection. Within this generic uniformity, various distinctive experience rooms are created with a view to attracting different target groups.

All experience rooms relate to the needs of everyday life – such as sleeping, cooking, working, and entertaining. For example, the living rooms are designed as representations of 'real' living rooms, with appropriate furniture, fabrics, lighting, books, televisions, and so on. It is sometimes the case that customers decide to buy all the items in the experience room because they can clearly envisage that specific living room as their own. Even when they do not buy everything, the rooms are a great source of inspiration. Many customers are inspired by new ideas while in the experience rooms, and their involvement, interaction, and communication are often intense.

Table 4.1   A summary of the five design dimensions of the experience room and the 'hyperreal' service

Design dimensions	Description
1. Physical artefacts	Physical attributes of the experience room: signs, symbols, and products
2. Intangible artefacts	Intangible attributes of the experience room: mental images, brand, and culture
3. Technology	The nature and role of technology
4. Customer placement	The 'staging' of the customer in the experience room
5. Customer involvement	The involvement of the customer in the experience
The 'hyperreal' service experience	The customer's interpretation of the 'hyperreal' service provided in the experience room

In addition to consulting IKEA staff, customers in experience rooms often discuss matters with one another. They also have access to a large database containing information about different sizes, colours, and so on.

Furniture can also be placed in an experience room that is the same size as the customer's room. This promotes an enhanced form of 'hyperreality' to illustrate solutions to real-life problems at home.

In a personal interview with the authors, an IKEA communications manager at regional level made the following observations about the IKEA approach to 'experience rooms':

> We have everything under one roof and we carefully create a space and show solutions to the customers ... to make their lives at home better [We show them] how they can set up their room, how they can arrange their furniture, how they can light up their room, [and we provide] tips and ideas about how they can improve their room. It can be a living room ... a kitchen or ... a bedroom... [all] different spaces within the house where we try to show how our expertise and products can create a better environment in their home ... We are able to do this because of the wide range of products that we are selling. We are able to put them together in an attractive way. We try to keep it fresh and thus provide a new experience to the customers every time. It is very much based on reality ... We try to be as close to reality as we can ... in a store.

The experience rooms combine functionality with emotional involvement to create a favourable customer experience. The 'hyperreality' is perceived to be true reality through a combination of furniture, decoration, and service. Both cognitive and affective mental faculties are involved in creating the experiences. It is not quite a real-life situation (or as IKEA puts it 'an everyday life situation') but the 'hyperreality' of the experience room does approximate to the customers' daily life experiences. The rooms provide inspiration, encourage interaction, and provoke discussion.

Design dimensions used by IKEA

Physical artefacts

The physical artefacts used by IKEA include furniture, fabrics, glasses, candles, plates, layout, and signs. These physical artefacts are utilised to create the illusion of being in the various rooms of a home. Space, light, and ambient temperature also contribute to this illusion.

Another role of the physical artefacts is to guide customers through the store and into the warehouse, where the products are picked up by the buyer before being taken to the checkout counter. Signage, coloured floor coverings, and variable intensities of lighting guide customers along the route through the store.

A third role is the provision of information about the products. Strategically placed information boards provide customers with detailed product-information labels, as do information labels on many of the products.

A fourth role of the physical artefacts is to provide customers and their families with tangible value in the form of refreshments and entertainment. Children can occupy themselves in a play area called *Småland* (which is named after IKEA's home province in Sweden, and which can also be interpreted as the 'land of the little people'). A restaurant provides Swedish-style food and drink. A fast-food area is also available to customers.

Intangible artefacts

The intangible artefacts utilised by IKEA include the organisation's image and brand, the catalogue, and the supporting activities, images, and themes. Although the catalogue is, strictly speaking, a tangible artefact, it also functions as an intangible artefact in the experience room because it depicts photographs of home interiors that provide strong mental images. The catalogue also communicates subtle messages about the IKEA brand and values, including the firm's commitment to social and environmental responsibility and low prices.

Images are presented in a contemporary design with good technical quality. Various themes are created in the experience rooms, and these are supported by the catalogues, commercials, and a loyalty programme.

Other intangible artefacts include the IKEA cultural values of informality, cost consciousness, responsibility, and humility. The organisation's culture is thus communicated to its customers through its intangible artefacts.

The intangible artefacts also demonstrate that IKEA has a deep under-standing of its customers and their needs. For example, IKEA designers are aware of the needs of a family with small children as they enter the house on a wet winter's afternoon. IKEA is aware of the need for a full range of entrance hall and storage furniture, appropriate carpets and textiles, and enough hangers to cater for wet raincoats, muddy shoes, and bags. IKEA studies its customers in their own reality to understand how it can add value to their lives (Ström and Tillberg, 2003). The experience room and its physical artefacts thus demonstrate the intangible artefact of thinking about customers' real needs (Edvardsson and Enquist, 2002).

A third role of the intangible artefacts is demonstrating IKEA's codes of conduct. For example, In the IKEA store in Milton Keynes (England), sustainability is an important intangible artefact. The store has been designed to have a minimal impact on the environment and to encourage customers and employees to live an 'environmentally friendly' life. Traditional single-use plastic bags have been replaced at the checkouts with recyclable bags. In the United Kingdom, IKEA uses only 'hybrid' cars (that is, cars with a combination of an electric motor and a petrol engine), and the company plans to implement this policy across the world in future. In these ways, the intangible artefact of IKEA's commitment to environmental sustainability is communicated to its customers.

Technology

Technology plays a key role in enabling customer involvement in the experience rooms at IKEA. An essential aspect of the utilisation of technology at IKEA is its application in the design of furniture such that customers can assemble the pieces at home. This provides value for customers by making transportation easier and reducing product costs.

Technology is also used in computer terminals that enable customers to search for products, colours, and other information. Computers are also used to help customers perform their own interior design by means of 3-D simulation.

The IKEA website is an important aspect of IKEA's use of technology. An increasing number of customers use the website, and the company has responded by placing more emphasis on 'meeting the customer' at the website and offering inspiration and solutions to those at home in front of the computer.

As IKEA's CEO, Anders Dahlvig, observed (quoted in Caplan, 2006, p. A10):

> In the past the Internet hasn't been an emphasis, but it will become a source of information to complement our stores on a totally different level. We have more than 200 million visitors to our website worldwide and more than 400 million visitors to our stores. In three years we'll have more visitors to the Net than to our stores.

An example of how IKEA is using Internet technology is its US website, on which a customer can browse through different kitchens and click on specific items to access more information. The website also has a 'virtual kitchen' where customers can enter the measurements of their own kitchens and see what they would look like with various pieces of IKEA furniture in position. The programme also provides the prices for the various alternatives.

IKEA also offers online 'experience rooms' on their various national websites, where customers can access more information about the different products.

Customer placement

The value of customer placement resides in allowing customers to immerse themselves in the 'hyperreal' service and create their own reality. At an IKEA store, people can sit in an experience room watching television and 'feeling at home' (Hagenaar and Hart, 2003). At the IKEA store in Beijing, China, customers have been seen to sleep for hours on a couch in a showroom, as reported in the following story (Paul and Yu, 2003):

> The first thing I noticed was how relaxed Chinese customers could be in an IKEA store [and] how much time they had ... [In] the living sofa department, kitchen furniture [department] and bedroom department – all seats on beds, chairs, or sofas were occupied. Friends and family members were sitting together and talked; exhausted customers had a nap, or people just sat and observed other customers.

An unusual example of placing people in an 'experience room' occurred in the Swedish city of Karlstad. As part of a campaign preceding the opening of a new store in this city, IKEA furnished the local railway station with furniture from the IKEA store – thus creating an 'experience room' outside the store. The campaign received a great deal of attention in the local media. This example shows how IKEA meets its customers by placing them in an IKEA experience room – even outside the actual store.

Customer involvement

The value of customer involvement in the IKEA 'experience room' resides in customers co-creating and assessing solutions to their particular needs at home. Customer involvement is also apparent in their interactions with one another, with employees, and with technology in co-creating these experiences. Interaction also takes place among children in the play areas, among customers who assist one another to find items in the warehouse, and through the sharing of ideas and suggestions during informal conversations.

It is important to note that customers are involved and that they create their own experiences, not pre-defined ones. However, customers are involved in a planned way in accordance with an open script similar to that used in improvisational theatre. The way IKEA presents itself to its customers in the catalogue is all about co-creating value, about how activities have been reallocated between provider and customer.

Customer involvement is also apparent in IKEA's 'Small Business Owners Guide' in the United States. This guide presents solutions to real-life problems in small businesses. IKEA also has a special website <www.business.ikea.com> for its US business customers. This website offers a 'Submit your space' section where business owners can submit pictures of how they have solved their furnishing problems, together with short comments on how they use IKEA furniture to create a better business atmosphere. This encourages customers to interact and inspire each other, thus enhancing customer involvement in helping each other. The website also has a voting system that enables customers to vote on the best solutions and ideas.

Another example of customer involvement can be found on a consumer website, <www.ikeafans.com>, which is run by people who are 'fans' of the store and its products. This website provides information about assembling furniture, as well as news, ideas, and other items connected with IKEA and its products. The site relies on interaction among visitors to the forum. The website also contains links to blogs where people post articles and pictures connected with IKEA. The website even has its own online store where it is possible to buy 'IKEAFANS' T-shirts and cards.

The 'hyperreal' service experience

At IKEA, the customers' 'hyperreal' experiences involve the co-creation of home solutions, assisted by family, staff, technology, and artefacts. The experience provides a low-risk pre-purchase assessment (physical, cognitive, and emotional) of the potential effects of a major purchase. Customer involvement is emphasised – not only directly in the experience room, but also through the IKEA loyalty programme, special offers, and the annual catalogue. Through customer involvement, customers create their own experiences, rather than entering pre-defined experiences.

Prahalad and Ramaswamy (2004) endorsed this practice of 'co-creating unique value with customers' in their notion of 'experience design', whereby the problem-solving skills and behaviour of provider and customer are incorporated into the product and service design to facilitate the co-construction of an individualised experience. Similarly, Schmitt's (2003) book, *Customer Experience Management*, promoted the desirability of 'analyzing the experimental world of the customer'. This approach is adopted by IKEA in its development of its products and service concepts. IKEA has developed a profound understanding of its customers and their everyday lives and needs.

Summary of design dimensions used by IKEA

Table 4.2 summarises the design dimensions used by IKEA and the principal roles played by each of the dimensions in creating value for the customer.

Two narratives

Two narratives illustrate how customers create their own unique experience by utilising an IKEA store as an 'experience room'.

A day at an IKEA store in the USA

On a cloudy Saturday in May, the Johnson family is planning a trip to the mall. Because they live near Chicago, they choose the Woodfield shopping mall in Schaumburg, one of the biggest malls in the US, as well as one of

Table 4.2   Design dimensions, examples, and roles used in co-creating customer value at IKEA

Design dimensions	Examples	Role in creating value
1. Physical artefacts	Furniture and fabrics, glasses, candles, plates, layout, signs	Host the experience room Guide customers through the process Provide information Provide tangible value
2. Intangible artefacts	Catalogue, supporting activities, images, themes	Provide information, ideas, and inspiration Represent brand, values, and culture Demonstrate understanding of customer needs
3. Technology	Self-assembly Computer search and design facilities	Ease of transportation Reduced costs Co-creating home solutions
4. Customer placement	Placing the customer in the experience rooms	Allow customers to immerse themselves in the hyperreal service and create their own reality
5. Customer involvement	Interaction and involvement with artefacts, family, staff, other customers	Co-creating and assessing solutions Co-creating the experience prior to purchase

the biggest tourist attractions near Chicago. Ben and Sandy have received a gift card for use at IKEA from their friends, so they also plan to go to the IKEA store.

Having arrived in Schaumburg they park their car at the Woodfield centre. They decide to go to the IKEA store first before moving on to other stores. Because they will do a lot of walking during the day they wait for the free transit service that will take them to the IKEA store. The IKEA building is easy to identify with its yellow and blue colours. The family has never visited IKEA previously and, judging by the appearance of the large building, they think it is a European variant of a shopping mall. Two greeters welcome the family members when they finally enter the store.

Ben Johnson begins talking with the employees while the children are becoming annoyed and hungry. Sandy asks where the shoe department is because she wants to buy some new shoes today and she knows that European brands are usually fashion 'trendy'. When she asks one of the greeters for the shoe department, the employees begin to laugh a little. They then explain that this is not an ordinary shopping mall. They explain that IKEA is a Swedish home-furniture dealer that also sells accessories. The greeter tells Sandy and Ben to take the escalator to the third floor so they can start their 'journey'.

When the family arrives at the top floor they are surprised at the space in the shop. The natural lighting gives the shop a unique ambience that the family has not experienced at any other store in the US. Ben looks at the kitchen section, where several showrooms display complete kitchen solutions. He thinks that it looks as if they have been taken out of a house and placed in the store. However, the children do not care much about the kitchen furniture and become annoyed. The family therefore decides to go to the restaurant, which is situated in the middle of the third floor.

When entering the restaurant they can look down over the railing and see all the other floors. The family realises that it is going to take a while to see the whole store. They take a seat in the restaurant while Ben walks to the kitchen and orders coffee, which has the weird name 'Löfbergs Lila'. He also buys some traditional Swedish snacks for the family.

While the adults are enjoying their Swedish coffee, the children notice that there is a play corner next to the restaurant. After their parents have finished their coffee, the children have a look at the children's corner, called 'Småland'. They immediately begin to play with other children and don't wish to leave. Ben and Sandy see this as an opportunity to walk through the store in peace and quietness, so they agree to pick up the children in one hour. Finally, Ben and Sandy can walk around at their own pace.

After walking around the third floor, they take the escalator down to the second floor. There they obtain a trolley to carry all the small things that

Sandy has already collected. She thinks that there are so many attractive and useful things at IKEA. While Sandy goes to the textile department to find some new curtains, Ben walks around the children's department to see if he can find something there. After walking around for a while, Ben gains a great deal of inspiration regarding the children's room. The children have been asking for a bunk for some time now, and Ben finds a bunk bed that would be perfect. Sandy returns. She has found some curtains, but she needs to measure at home before she purchases them. After seeing all the solutions for the children's room, Ben and Sandy agree that they want to redecorate the children's rooms at home. They already have some ideas what to buy, but they first want to ask the children for their opinion.

When they arrive at 'Småland', they find it difficult to get the children to leave the playground. But when the parents tell the children that they plan a 'new' bedroom, they race out of 'Småland' to the colourful children's department. After an hour of testing various ideas, the family finally know what to buy – which is somewhat more realistic than what the children wanted in the first place (which would have fitted in the sleeping room if it was 10 times larger!).

The family contacts one of the IKEA co-workers in the store. She explains to the family that they can pick up the selected pre-packed items from the warehouse and that they can take them home today and assemble them. Because the family does not have space in the car for all the items that they have selected, they decide to have the articles delivered; and because Ben and Sandy both have busy jobs, they decide to arrange for an assembly service as well.

After completing their purchases, they realise that they have spent the whole day at IKEA. The children are feeling hungry again, so the family goes to the IKEA restaurant again. This time they eat Swedish meatballs and other traditional Swedish dishes. The children are excited about their new room. Before they leave the store, Ben buys some packs of the Swedish coffee ('Löfbergs Lila') to take home with him.

A day at an IKEA store in China

Wang Ming and Li Xiang are a couple in their mid-20s who live in downtown Shanghai. Ming works as an accountant and Xiang is a writer for a fashion magazine. They have just moved into a new apartment and are now looking to buy some furniture for it. They are familiar with traditional Chinese furniture, but they both agree that they don't want to have the same furnishings as their parents. It is important for Xiang to have a home that shows her unique personality and distinguishes her from her friends.

Xiang heard about IKEA from friends and she feels that the IKEA catalogue is like a fashion magazine. Before they leave for the IKEA store, Xiang goes through the catalogue, making notes and coming up with ideas for their own home. Ming prefers to use the IKEA website because he finds it more visually effective.

Because they don't own a car, Ming and Xiang take public transport to the IKEA supermarket. A large public transport guide, written in both Chinese and in English, makes it easy for Ming and Xiang to rely on public transport to reach the store.

The Shanghai store has three floors. The first floor is the market hall, the second floor has the showrooms, and the ground floor is for parking. On entering the store, Ming and Xiang look at the showroom in the centre of the hall. Designers at IKEA change this showroom frequently. A range of products priced at about 59 Yuan, which is a low price, is the first experience for customers to observe. Customers are then expected to go upstairs using the elevator.

When Ming and Xiang reach the second floor they see the various showrooms. They make their way to the 'miniature apartments' to see the solutions that IKEA has suggested for small spaces. Because Ming and Xiang have a small apartment, it is important for them to buy furniture that is both attractive and functional. On a bulletin board near the showrooms the customers can read about saving space in their apartments. Ming takes a seat on a sofa in a showroom while Xiang walks around and writes down measurements and details of where they can find the items they want to buy. They can touch and read about every item in the showrooms, and they can also find information about the materials used in constructing various pieces of furniture and where the items can be found in the warehouse. They both admire the environmentally friendly material used in the furniture, especially the natural wood that is used in so many of the products.

Managerial implications for other companies

The value for customers of a pre-purchase service experience

IKEA has demonstrated the broad spectrum of value-in-use that can be provided to customers during a pre-purchase service experience. The benefits include:

- the provision of inspiration;
- the encouragement of interaction, involvement, and discussion;
- guiding customers towards information throughout the process;
- communication of tangible values and intangible values;

- exposure to the organisation's brand and values; and
- enabling the co-creation of an experience.

As demonstrated in this chapter, service organisations can create value for their customers through the co-creation of values-based service experiences. This value is created while simultaneously reducing risk for the customer and increasing their imaginative interaction with the organisation. The dimensions of the 'experience room' presented in this chapter provide a starting point for a discussion of what value should be provided and how this might be achieved. The example of IKEA provides stimulus and guidance to other organisations that might be considering the development of pre-purchase experiences.

Hyperreal service but real service experience

'Hyperreality' can be used to provide customers with a pre-purchase service experience. The aims are: (i) to add unique and personalised value to the service; (ii) to connect with the customer by means of exposure to the organisation's norms and values; (iii) to create a unique identity; (iv) to increase loyalty and sales; (v) to manage customer expectations regarding quality-in-use; and (vi) to learn more about customers' needs and desires for the purposes of service development and quality improvement.

Just as product-based organisations can usually enable their customers to 'test drive' their products, service organisations can facilitate a 'test drive' of services – albeit in a simulated or 'hyperreal' manner. Based on the case study of IKEA and a review of the literature, such a 'hyperreal' pre-purchase experience should enable customers to (Edvardsson *et al.*, 2005):

- relate to the service situation and their own personal needs/situation;
- test, assess, and measure the physical, functional, and cognitive attributes of the desired service;
- test and assess the experience and emotions involved in the service;
- co-create and experience the simulated service for themselves;
- involve others (such as family and friends) in the co-creation; and
- reduce the risk involved in making the purchase.

Designing the experience room

An 'experience room' enables customers to 'test-drive' a service before purchase, use and consumption. It is important not to create unrealistic expectations; rather, the focus should be on issues and service dimensions of greatest importance to the customers. The experience room must be flexible and easy for the customers to use or manage.

The framework of five dimensions of an 'experience room' presented here has been tested in several service contexts – including buying a new house, designing a homepage for a research conference, and deciding on an MBA programme at a business school (Edvardsson *et al.*, 2007). These tests indicated that the design dimensions are appropriate in describing and analysing the design of a pre-purchase service experience in these contexts. These tests also demonstrated that customer involvement should be facilitated by the deliberate design of potential customer-to-customer interaction. Customers can learn much from one another and can enrich the service experience in many contexts.

Questions

1   What is most important for your customers when assessing a service before purchase and consumption?
2   What is complicated for you to describe (and for the customer to understand) about the services being offered in your company?
3   How can your customers be more involved in co-designing their own services?
4   How is the experience room designed today in your company?
5   How can you develop an experience room and make it easier for your customers to test-drive your service?
6   What can you learn from the example of how IKEA creates experience rooms and enables customers to test-drive their services?
7   What opportunities do three-dimensional Internet facilities (such as 'second life') offer your company with regard to creating test-drives for customers?

References

Arnould, E.E., Price, L.L. and Tierney, P. (1998) Communicative staging of the wilderness servicescape, *The Service Industries Journal*, Vol. 18, No. 3, pp. 90–115.

Bendapudi, N. and Leone, R.P. (2003) Psychological implications of customer participation on co-production, *Journal of Marketing*, Vol. 67, January, pp. 14–28.

Berry, L., Carbone, L. and Haeckel, S. (2002) Managing the total customer experience, *MIT Sloan Management Review*, Vol. 43, No 3, pp. 85–9.

Bitner, M.J. (1992) Servicescapes: the impact of physical surroundings on customers and employees, *Journal of Marketing*, Vol. 56, April, pp. 57–71.

Caplan, J. (2006) 'Quick change artist', *Time Bonus Section*, July 2006, A8–A10.

Cronin, J. (2003) Looking back to see forward in services marketing: some ideas to consider, *Managing Service Quality*, Vol. 13. No. 5, pp. 332–7.

Edvardsson, B. and Enquist, B. (2002) The IKEA SAGA – how service culture drives service strategy, *The Service Industries Journal*, Vol. 22, No. 4, pp. 153–86.

Edvardsson, B., Enquist, B. and Johnston, B. (2005) Co-creating customer value through hyperreality in the pre-purchase service experience, *Journal of Service Research*, Vol. 8, No. 2, pp. 149–61.

Edvardsson, B., Enquist, B. and Johnston, B. (2007) 'Creating and test-driving service experience prior to purchase and consumption'. Paper presented at QUIS10, Orlando, June 11–14.

Hagenaar, B. and Hart, A. (2003) From 'Köttbullar till Bokhyllor': a study concerning the customer experience at IKEA Kungens Kurva. Master's thesis, Karlstad University, Sweden.

IKEA (2005) *IKEA Social and Environmental Responsibility Report*. Corporate PR, IKEA Services AB.

IKEA (2007a) 'Grönare Liv', *IKEA Family Live*, Autumn, 2007, pp. 62–3 (in Swedish).

IKEA (2007b) 'IKEA checks out of plastic bags', press release, IKEA UK, 9 July.

Johnston, R. and Clark, G. (2001) *Service Operations Management*. London: Prentice Hall.

Mano, H. and Oliver, R.L. (1993) Assessing the dimensionality and structure of the consumption experience: evaluation, feeling, and satisfaction, *Journal of Consumer Research*, Vol. 20, December, pp. 451–66.

Normann, R. (2001) *Reframing Business: When the Map Changes the Landscape*. New York: John Wiley.

Park, W. and Young, S.M. (1984) *The Effects of Involvement and Executional Factors of a Television Commercial on Brand Attitude Formation*. Report No. 84-100, Marketing Science Institute, Cambridge, MA.

Paul, V. and Yu, B. (2003) Towards a long-run perspective driven by value-based service culture: a case study of IKEA in China. Master's thesis, Karlstad University, Sweden.

Prahalad, C.K. and Ramaswamy, V. (2004) *The Future of Competition: Co-Creating Unique Value with Customers*. Boston, MA: Harvard Business School Press.

Schmitt, B.H. (2003) *Customer Experience Management*. New York: John Wiley.

Shaw, C. and Ivens, J. (2002) *Building Great Customer Experiences*. London: Palgrave.

Sherry, J., Jr. (ed.) (1998) *ServiceScapes: The Concept of Place in Contemporary Market*. Chicago, IL: American Marketing Association.

Ström, L. and Tillberg, E. (2003) *Smart Tillväxt Kunddriven förändring i företag och organisationer*. Stockholm: Ekerlids (in Swedish).

Swaminathan, V., Zinkhan, G.M. and Reddy, S.K. (1996) The evolution and antecedents of transformational advertising: a conceptual model, *Advances in Consumer Research*, Vol. 23, No. 1, pp. 49–55.

Vargo, S.L. and Lusch, R.F. (2004) Evolving to a new dominant logic of marketing, *Journal of Marketing*, 68 (January), pp. 1–17.

Venkatesh, A. (1999) Postmodernism perspectives for macromarketing: an inquiry into the global information and sign economy, *Journal of Macromarketing*, Vol. 18, No. 2, pp. 153–69.

Voss, C. (2003) *The Experience Profit Cycle*. Research report, Center for Operations and Technology Management, London Business School, London.

5 Values-based service brands and marketing communication

Introduction

The essential role of brands is to differentiate a company or a service from others in satisfying a given customer need. The differentiating characteristics represented by the brand can be functional (cognitive) or symbolic (emotional). The term 'brand equity' refers to the value added to products and services by a brand; such brand equity is derived from the way in which consumers respond to the brand in terms of their thinking, feelings, and actions.

This chapter focuses on how organisational values relate to service brand management and marketing communication. The aim is to present a framework for values-based service brands and marketing communication using IKEA as an illustration (Edvardsson *et al.*, 2006). The chapter explores how values build a brand and how the brand can be used as a marketing vehicle to communicate values and reach out to customers and other stakeholders. The chapter discusses how vision, mission, corporate identity, image, and 'living the brand' are related to values in the globalised market context.

The chapter begins with a theoretical discussion of the issues involved and a summary of IKEA's marketing communication strategy, with particular emphasis on the brand. The chapter then presents a model for values-based service brands in action, including a discussion of how IKEA has developed and used its service brand to communicate core values in various marketing campaigns, its customer club, and its catalogue. The chapter ends with a summary of the insights to be gained from IKEA's use of its brand and the managerial implications for other companies.

Values-based management, corporate identity, and service brand

According to Hatch and Schultz (2001), a successful brand strategy requires the alignment of three essential elements:

- *vision:* which represents senior management's aspirations for the company;
- *culture:* which refers to the values, behaviours, and attitudes that reflect how employees feel about the company they are working for; and
- *image:* which is the impression of the company held by customers and other stakeholders (including the media and the shareholders).

Simones *et al.* (2005, p. 153) argued that corporate identity forms the basis for brands, and that values are a key component of corporate identity: 'Creating a strong corporate identity and image is a way for companies to encourage positive attitudes towards their organization'. Such an identity can be viewed as a 'vehicle' by which a company's character is conveyed to customers and other stakeholders. In this regard, brand identity has been referred to as the brand's distinctive 'fingerprint' (Upshaw, 1995). Aaker (1996, p. 68) defined brand identity as '… a unique set of brand associations that the brand strategist aspires to create or maintain'. Simones *et al.* (2005, p. 156) emphasised that the core component of brand identity is '… its "soul", brand values, and underpinning beliefs'. In a similar vein, Ind (2004, p. 13) argued that: '… a corporate brand is more than just the outward manifestation of an organization – its name, logo, visual presentation. Rather it is the core of values that defines it.' Values are thus vital to directing a company's activities (de Chernatony, 1999).

In service organisations, brand can also play an important role in helping customers to assess value before purchase and consumption. As Berry (2000, p. 18) noted:

> Strong brands enable customers to better visualize and understand intangible products. They reduce customers' perceived monetary, social, or safety risk in buying services, which are difficult to evaluate prior to purchase.

According to Keller (1999), the way in which a brand is communicated and explained is critical to the employees' internalisation of the brand. Corporate communication can be orchestrated by a sustainable 'corporate narrative' (van Riel, 2000). Berry and Bendapudi (2003) talked about 'clueing-in customers' and demonstrated how the corporate story of the Mayo Clinic in the USA involved sending the right service signals through 'clues in people', 'clues in collaboration', and 'clues in tangible'. Haeckel *et al.* (2003) also observed that 'delivering' the brand is connected with communicating the core values of the company.

Keller (1999) identified ten attributes that characterise the world's strongest brands. Among others, these attributes included: (i) that the brand excels at delivering the benefits consumers truly desire; (ii) that pricing is based on consumers' perceptions of value; (iii) that the brand is consistent; and (iv) that the brand is given proper and sustained support by the business.

As Kotler and Keller (2005, p. 276) observed: 'Brand equity is an important intangible asset that has psychological and financial value to the firm'. According to Aaker (1996), brand identity is particularly important for building brand equity. Ind (2004) emphasised the importance of 'living' the brand – which has to do with 'living up to' norms and values in various ways – for example, how employees interact with customers, how internal relationships are conducted, and how relationships with suppliers and partners are maintained. According to this view, the culture forms a basis for the 'living brand'. Brands thus communicate the values of an organisation to customers in creating a distinct and favourable image. A service brand can often equate with the whole company, which implies that the service becomes the corporate image.

Berry (1999) studied service companies that had been successful in the long term, and concluded that values and employee commitment provide energy and direction to such organisations. Value and values are co-produced with the customers (as well as with the other stakeholders) and expressed through the brand and marketing communication activities. Berry developed a service-branding model, which differed from a goods-branding model in that human performance and values were seen to play a critical role in building the brand in labour-intensive businesses, such as services. A well-developed brand evokes specific emotional resonances, and does so consistently with each customer's experience. Brand designers and marketers carefully choose emotions based on the 'personality' that the brand should establish, and the business goals behind it. Brands often try to create connections to the deeply rooted psycho-personal concepts and constructs that shape basic ways of thinking and feeling. Brands thus attempt to become associated with such constructs as 'identity' and 'lifestyle'; in the case of IKEA, the key association is 'home'.

IKEA's marketing communications strategy

The IKEA vision and business idea provide a framework for all IKEA marketing communications worldwide.

- The IKEA vision is: 'To create a better everyday life for the majority of people.'
- The IKEA business idea is: 'To offer a wide range of well-designed, functional home furnishing products at prices so low that as many people as possible will be able to afford them.'
- The IKEA market positioning statement (derived from the vision and business idea) is: 'Your partner in better living. We do our part; you do yours. Together we save money.'

The IKEA brand is the sum total of the emotional and cognitive values that consumers associate with the IKEA trademark and the reputation of the company. The brand image is the result of more than 50 years work by IKEA co-workers at all levels all over the world. An IKEA document of 2006 summarised the brand image in the following terms:

> What we do, what we say, the products we offer, the price we offer them at, the presentation of our range, and the information we provide our customers – all contribute to our image. The overall task of IKEA's marketing communication is to build the IKEA brand and inspire people to come to the stores.

IKEA's marketing communication has traditionally focused on printed media, which has proved to be very successful in communicating the firm's values over the years. The IKEA catalogue remains the main marketing tool, with approximately 70 per cent of the annual marketing budget being spent on this alone. The catalogue is produced in 56 different editions, in 27 languages for 44 countries, and more than 191 million catalogues were circulated in 2008. Despite this continuing emphasis on printed media, other media (including television, radio, and the internet) are now increasingly being utilised. Nevertheless, the IKEA store continues to be the primary medium for IKEA retailers to present their offerings, low prices, and the overall IKEA concept. The various forms of IKEA advertising and public relations are essentially *complementary* to the IKEA product range and store.

The IKEA brand is built on associations with cost-consciousness, design sensibility, unconventionality, and environmental awareness. For many customers, these associations form a basis of a general outlook and set of priorities for life in general. Indeed, these associations produce customer loyalty that borders on 'cult-like' blind devotion. Some retail customers have been known to camp outside new IKEA stores for weeks to win store-opening prizes of modest value.

A model of values-based service brands in action

The IKEA values that underlie the brand can be categorised as *economic, social,* and *environmental.* These values differentiate the IKEA brand – not only in terms of the sentiments expressed, but also in the words and styles that are used to communicate them to customers. IKEA challenges the established order and ways of thinking. In doing so, communication is more than a tool for transmitting values; rather, the communication is a 'value' in itself. There is evidence of strong bonds being formed between the brand and customers, and between the brand and various other stakeholders (such as co-workers and suppliers of IKEA).

IKEA's marketing focuses on customer value by communicating how customers can co-create solutions to real-life problems at home and thus promote a better life. Advertising in the catalogue, brochures, and the website all communicate this value proposition. The focus is not on the furniture *per se*; rather, the emphasis is on the value that can be realised by customers who utilise the offered resources in a personalised fashion to provide solutions to their own distinctive real-life problems. This approach is in accordance with Holbrook (2006), who argued that customer value is 'interactive' and 'relativistic'. According to Holbrook (2006), value is: (i) *comparative* (because it depends on the relative merits of one object as opposed to another); (ii) *situational* (because it varies from one customer context to another); and (iii) *personal* (because it differs from one individual to the next). *Customer value* thus resides in an *individual* consumption experience; and, for IKEA, *home* is the key concept in this individual consumption experience.

In service businesses, it is important to train, empower, and reward employees in such a way that they are able and willing to 'live the brand' when interacting with customers, suppliers, other partners, the mass media, and owners (Ind, 2004). Human performance plays a crucial role in building a service brand, and there must be a good fit between a firm's internal perspective and its external perspective (Berry, 1999; Grönroos, 2000; Ind, 2004). In this regard, core values are extremely important in sustaining the brand.

The proposed model of values-based service is shown in Figure 5.1. This model is based on a literature review, interviews with senior executives of IKEA, content analysis of company documents (such as 'The IKEA Way', 'IWAY' and 'A Furniture Dealer's Testament') and marketing campaigns. The model, which has been previously published in *Managing Service Quality* (Edvardsson *et al.*, 2006), posits that a dynamic brand is grounded in values that are understood and accepted by leaders and co-workers, and expressed through marketing communication.

At the centre of the model are the core values of the company. The drivers of the IKEA values-based service brand are: (i) low price (in relation to

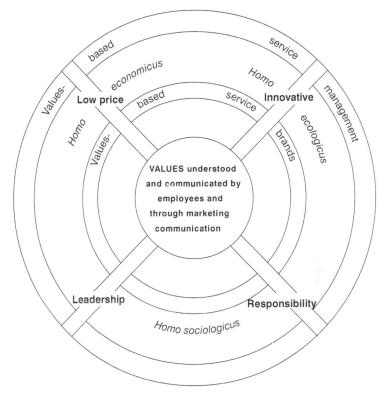

Figure 5.1 A model of values-based service brands in action (This figure first appeared in *Managing Service Quality,* Vol. 16, No. 3 (2006), pp. 230–46)

functional and design quality); (ii) innovative thinking and development; (iii) leadership that is visible, action-oriented, and directed by the core norms and values of the company culture; and (iv) responsibility (including corporate social and environmental responsibility). The role of the brand is to express these values internally (to co-workers) and externally (to customers, media, and other stakeholders).

In addition, the brand can also help in managing complaints and the service-recovery process, give direction for strategy development, and provide impetus for product development.

Value is co-created through IKEA's distinctive corporate and service culture to strengthen IKEA's service brand identity around the world. The values communicated to customers and other stakeholders are deeply rooted in IKEA's organisational culture and heritage. Moreover, the values are understood, accepted, and nurtured by co-workers and expressed through marketing communication.

Without low and competitive prices (in relation to functional and design quality), it is impossible to sell solutions to real-life problems at home to the majority of people. Consequently, the price tag comes first. In addition, solutions must be designed, produced, and delivered in accordance with environmental responsibilities, and must live up to high ethical standards and social responsibilities. It is essential to communicate the right message in the right way.

IKEA is often quite provocative in the way that it reaches out to customers, challenges them, and encourages them to respond. Words and expressions that are loaded with values are often used. The values expressed during communication play an important role in forming the corporate identity and the service brand. Examples are: 'democratic design'; 'stand by the side of the majority of people'; 'real-life problems'; and 'home: the most important place in the world'.

As previously noted, the focus is not on the physical products (the furniture), but on values and the service touching people. The values are communicated through various forms of advertising and publicity – including the catalogue, the website, the IKEA customer club, and in IKEA stores through direct interaction between customers and co-workers.

Values-based market communication and brand-building in IKEA

Democratic design

In developing the notion of 'democratic design', Ingvar Kamprad had addressed his own rhetorical questions: 'Why must well-designed furniture always be so expensive? Why do the most famous designers always fail to reach the majority of people with their ideas?' Kamprad noted that well-designed products (including furniture products) appeared to be only for the rich and privileged; in contrast, the multitude of people with less money were excluded. Kamprad's response to this unsatisfactory situation was to offer a wide range of home furnishings of good design and functionality at a price low enough to be affordable to most people. This idea of 'democratic design' had its natural genesis in IKEA's roots in the poor farming communities of the county of Småland in Sweden.

The three dimensions of 'democratic design' are form, functionality, and low price. With respect to the third dimension – low price – IKEA designers are always asked to use design to decrease prices, not increase them. In effect, the price tag is 'designed' first – beginning with a decision on what price the majority of people can afford to pay. A production line is then designed to produce furnishings that satisfy the other two dimensions.

To achieve this, designers work on the factory floor with production staff, rather than in a prestigious office in a distant city.

The notion of 'democratic design' was first proclaimed at the Milan Design Fair of 1995. Members of the public flocked to the IKEA exhibition, the Italian media provided much publicity, and consumers visited IKEA's stores in unprecedented numbers to buy 'democratically designed' furnishings. Since then, the concept of 'democratic design' has continued to be integral to the IKEA concept. This is apparent in the development of the rocking chair known as 'Lilleberg', in which designers used materials other than hard wood, and eliminated as much material as possible to make the package smaller. In the case of the heating candle known as 'Lampan', designers used long-lasting porcelain material. For the 'Gullholmen' chair, the designer weaved banana leaves together and thus demonstrated that raw materials that were previously perceived as waste can be used productively. Finally, the furniture series known as 'Jokkmokk' is made only from wood that is sourced from sustainable forestry practices conducted in accordance with strict environmental guidelines.

According to IKEA (2008): 'No-one should have to pay a high price for good function, quality, and design; and neither should the environment'.

'Chuck out the chintz!'

In 1997, St Luke's was a small (but energetic) advertising agency in London (UK). St Luke's was asked by IKEA to undertake a radical change in IKEA's image in the UK. The agency's marketing analysis revealed that 60 per cent of the market was traditionally minded and disliked anything foreign and new, including IKEA. A smaller proportion (30 per cent) of the market was more innovative, and might like IKEA. The remaining 10 per cent were undecided. St Luke's strategy was to allow the 'traditional' 60 per cent of the market to dislike IKEA to an even greater degree, induce the 30 per cent to like IKEA to a greater degree, and encourage the 10 per cent undecided to make a decision.

The main barrier was style. Many people who lived in small terraced homes covered their walls and floors (and even their toilet seats and toilet-paper holders) with flowery-patterned coverings – commonly referred to as 'chintz'. Many people also filled their already crowded homes with fake antiques – another form of 'chintz'. St Luke's launched a television advertising campaign with the slogan: 'Chuck out the chintz!' This advocated a more 'modern' style that would give people a new identity and change the homes of Britain. Blue-and-yellow waste-disposal 'skips' were placed in the streets for people to discard their 'chintz'.

The campaign had the desired effect. IKEA was transformed from being a strange foreign company to being a fashionable name that reached into the private lives of Britons in their homes. The television commercials ran only once, but for years afterwards people referred to the slogan 'chuck out the chintz', and associated it with IKEA.

Outlooking

As noted above, IKEA 'designs' the price tag first. The company decides how much a product should cost to make it affordable to most consumers. The product is then designed to achieve this low price while maintaining excellent function and good quality. The designer works on the factory floor to find the best solution at the best price. An example of this process was the company's 'LACK' range, which was initially a door produced by a manufacturer in Poland. The door was placed horizontally on a trestle to become a table. It was then cut into pieces to produce shelves. These were then subdivided into coffee tables. The pieces were then placed horizontally and vertically to become bookshelves. The resulting 'board-on-frame' construction used only 30 per cent of the energy and materials required to produce tables. Moreover, it could be packed flat, was light, and saved space in transport. This combination of qualities was considered environmentally friendly, and the product was placed in IKEA stores. The price to the consumer of a 'LACK' table is now only about 30 per cent of its original price in 1990. The production volume in the past 15 years has increased approximately ten-fold.

'Be brave, not beige!'

IKEA now inspires American customers to invest in their homes with the campaign slogan 'Be brave not beige!' – a similar campaign to the successful 'chuck out the chintz' campaign in the UK. The campaign was launched in 2007 and has its own website <www.bebravenotbeige.com>, which is connected to IKEA's American website. On the campaign website, customers can change the colours of furniture in various showrooms. The website also enables customers to experiment with different combinations of furniture. The aim is to inspire website visitors to make changes in their own homes.

The website also includes videos of older people undertaking activities usually associated with younger folk – such as an older woman playing the drums in a room decorated with IKEA furniture, or an older man doing gymnastic exercises accompanied by energetic pop music.

These examples illustrate IKEA's desire to meet their customers in innovative ways. The campaign has stimulated a great deal of online 'chat', and influential blogs have posted links to the various videos and praised the inventive and easy-to-use website.

'Stay home today!'

Because women have significant influence in making decisions about the purchase of interior decoration in Japanese households, IKEA focused on female customers when launching its concept in Japan. The IKEA advertising campaign used such slogans as: 'The home is the most important place in the world'; 'Have you seen your kids today?'; and 'Stay home today!' These advertisements were rather controversial in Japan; indeed, one railway company refused to use the advertisements on billboards on the grounds that the advertising message encouraged people to stay home from work. However, the advertising campaign did achieve its purpose in communicating the message that IKEA planned to change the *status quo* in the Japanese furniture market.

IKEA also opened a children's day-care centre at its store to make it easier for women with children to work at IKEA. The rationale was to assist women who had children to be able to get back into working life, which can be difficult to achieve in Japan because the government's scheme for children's day care is rather weak.

To ensure that Japanese people understood the IKEA concept, the company organised exhibitions to showcase 'compact living'. This involved the placement of various 'boxes' around cities to demonstrate what can be achieved in a small Japanese apartment with IKEA furniture.

IKEA undertook a great deal of market research and careful preparation before opening its first store in Japan in 2006. As the CEO, Anders Dahlvig, observed (*Time*, 2006):

> We spent five years planning. We had to find a site, and then there were regulations to adapt to, and customs duties. And we had to understand how Japanese people live. We looked at 100 homes. We sat down with people and asked: 'What do you do? Where do your kids sleep? How do you work and play with them?'

IKEA has made quite significant changes to its concept to suit the needs of Japanese customers; indeed, the modifications to the basic IKEA concept have been greater than those put in place in any other country that IKEA has entered in recent years. In particular, the concept of self-assembly (of furniture) is apparently a significant obstacle for Japanese customers; in response to this, IKEA's home-delivery and assembling services have been enhanced. Moreover, IKEA also offers to take away their customers' old furniture.

In general, IKEA is making a significant effort to educate customers through furniture exhibitions and special brochures (both at the store, and elsewhere).

'One-tenth of all Europeans have been made in one of these'

IKEA entered Russia during an economic crisis that had forced several other foreign companies to leave the country. However, IKEA took advantage of several favourable factors associated with the economic downturn – including decreased manufacturing costs, depressed land prices, and the ready availability of skilled labour.

The work of building the image of IKEA in Russia was entrusted to a Moscow-based advertising firm, BBDO, which developed a campaign that was designed to provoke a reaction among consumers and communicate the fact that IKEA is not an ordinary company. One advertisement had a picture of a bed from IKEA with the text: 'One-tenth of all Europeans have been made in one of these'. The slogan was too controversial for the transport authority, which banned the commercial. Nevertheless, this ban ensured that IKEA received a great deal of free attention in the media (Torekull, 2003).

IKEA Family

'IKEA Family' is the name of IKEA's customer club. One-fifth of IKEA's customers are responsible for 60–70 per cent of total turnover, and these people frequent IKEA's stores three times as often as do other customers. It is for these people that the customer club exists.

The club had existed in a few countries in various guises since the mid-1980s, but in 2005 a new version was introduced in Sweden, Denmark, Austria, France, Germany, and Italy. By 2007, 'IKEA Family' was established in all IKEA stores. The club does not aim to recruit new customers; rather, it has three main aims: (i) to strengthen members' ties with IKEA; (ii) to encourage them to visit IKEA stores and the website more often; and (iii) to increase turnover across the entire IKEA range.

Unlike many other customer clubs, 'IKEA Family' does not have a bonus system; rather it is about customer feedback and involvement in improving products. According to the head of the 'IKEA Family' (quoted in Enquist *et al.*, 2007):

Customers join because they have an interest in interiors and feel that IKEA contributes to improving their life at home. 'IKEA Family' offers are more about knowledge and activities than collecting bonus points … Profits from store sales are put towards 'IKEA Family' activities at local stores. The more products that are sold, the more activities can be organised. This, in turn, leads to increased sales across the whole IKEA range.

Insights from IKEA: Brand and marketing implications for other companies

Vision, culture, and image

It is apparent from the above discussion that three essential elements – *vision, culture,* and *image* – must be aligned in a successful values-based branding strategy. In IKEA's marketing, value-in-use for customers is mainly of an instrumental nature. However, there is also communication beyond the instrumental level; indeed, strong bonds are formed between the brand and customers, and between the brand and various other stakeholders (such as co-workers and suppliers of IKEA). The IKEA marketing strategy incorporates a successful branding strategy in which *vision, culture,* and *image* are complementary.

Market positioning

The brand is the sum total of the emotional and cognitive values that consumers associate with the brand and the reputation of the company. Values cannot easily be linked to individual products; rather, it is necessary to link them with corporate identity and the customers' broader perceptions of the company. These values then provide direction for the customers in making decisions and reducing risk. The brand thus comes to embody and express the values that add to customer value-in-use.

In contrast, if companies are linked to negative values (such as child labour, pollution, and unethical conduct), this will reduce value-in-use for the customers. Customers have expectations with respect to corporate values, and a failure to meet these expectations will have an adverse impact on customers' perceptions of total value; this, in turn, has implications for loyalty and profitability.

Choosing a few attractive values

To be successful and sustainable, a company needs to focus on a few values that are attractive to its customers, employees, and other stakeholders. Such values as ethical social behaviour and environmental responsibility are likely to create 'values resonance' (rather than 'values dissonance') with these vital stakeholders.

In this regard, the IKEA brand is built on associations with cost-consciousness, sensible design, unconventionality, and social and environmental awareness. Customers who furnish their homes with IKEA's products are demonstrating (to themselves and others) that these associations represent an outlook and a set of priorities for life in general. In this way, a values-based branding strategy connects to life at home and contributes to a better life for customers.

Living the brand

In service businesses, it is important to train, empower, and reward employees, so that they are able and willing to 'live the brand' when interacting with one another, customers, suppliers, other partners, the mass media, and owners. Human performance plays a crucial role in building a service and values-based brand, and there must be a good fit between a firm's internal perspective and its external perspective. In this regard, core values are extremely important in sustaining the brand.

'Living the brand' is about role models, storytelling, and trying new ways of developing the brand and communicating with customers and other stakeholders. Living the IKEA brand is learnt through on-the-job daily training, as well as in educational programmes that explain and teach the IKEA way.

'Living the brand' is also transferred to new markets and new stores in a systematic manner. The values of the IKEA culture drive the overall brand strategy, the ongoing internal corporate narrative, the advertising programmes, and in the myriad other tools that are utilised in IKEA's marketing activities.

Questions

1   What values are focused on in brand-building?
2   How is marketing communication aligned with the business idea, organisational culture, and business strategy?
3   What creates customer value and what destroys value?
4   What do you want your brand to be associated with?

5 How is your brand perceived and assessed among customers and other stakeholders?
6 How do you ensure that employees and leaders 'live the brand'?
7 What roles do economic, social, and environmental values play in brand-building and marketing communication?
8 How can you challenge the established values in a way that attracts customers and creates a sustainable business?

References

Aaker, D.A. (1996) *Building Strong Brands*. New York: The Free Press.

Berry, L.L. (1999) *Discovering the Soul of Service*. New York: The Free Press.

Berry, L.L. (2000) Cultivating service brand equity, *Journal of the Academy of Marketing Science*, Vol. 28, No. 1, pp. 128–37.

Berry, L.L. and Bendapudi, N. (2003) Clueing in customers, *Harvard Business Review*, Vol. 81, No. 2, pp. 100–6.

Edvardsson, B. and Enquist, B. (2002) 'The IKEA SAGA' – service culture drives service strategy, *The Service Industries Journal*, Vol. 22, No. 4, pp. 153–86.

Edvardsson, B., Enquist, B. and Hay, M. (2006) Values-based service brands: narratives from IKEA, *Managing Service Quality*, Vol. 16, No. 3, pp. 230–46.

Enquist, B., Edvardsson, B. and Petros S.S. (2007) Values based service quality for sustainable business, *Managing Service Quality*, Vol. 17, No. 4, pp. 385–403.

Grönroos, C. (2000) *Service Management and Marketing – A Customer Relationship Management Approach*, 2nd edition. Chichester: Wiley.

Haeckel, S.H., Carbone, L.P. and Berry, L.L. (2003) How to lead the customer experience, *Marketing Management*, Vol. 12, No. 1, pp. 18–24.

Hatch, M.J. and Schultz, M. (2001) Are the strategic stars aligned for your corporate brand?, *Harvard Business Review*, Vol. 79, No. 2, pp. 128–34.

Holbrook, M.B. (2006) ROSEPEKICECIVEC versus CCV, in R.F. Lusch and S.L. Vargo (eds), *The Service-Dominant Logic of Marketing*. New York: M.E. Sharpe.

IKEA (2008) IKEA Catalogue 2008, Swedish edition.

Ind, N. (2004) *Living The Brand*, 2nd edn. New York: Kogan Page.

Keller, K.L. (1999) Managing brands for the long run: reinforcement and revitalization strategies, *California Management Review*, Vol. 41, No. 3, Spring, pp. 102–24.

Kotler, P. and Keller, K.L. (2005) *Marketing Management, 12e*. New York: Prentice-Hall.

Van Riel, C.B.M. (2000) Corporate communication orchestrated by a sustainable corporate story, in M. Schultz, M.J. Hatch and M.H. Larsen (eds), *The Expressive Organization. Linking Identity, Reputation, and the Corporate Brand*. Oxford: Oxford University Press.

Simones, C., Dibb, S. and Fisk, R.P. (2005) Managing corporate identity: an internal perspective, *Journal of the Academy of Marketing Science*, Vol. 33, No. 2, pp. 153–68.

Torekull, B. (1999) *Leading by Design: The IKEA Story*. New York: Harper Business.

Torekull, B. (2003) *Historien om IKEA*. 2nd edn. Stockholm: Wahlström & Widstrand.

Upshaw, L. (1995) The key to building cyberbrands, *Advertising Age*, Vol. 66, No. 22, May, pp. 18–29.

6 Values-based service leadership

Introduction

Ethical corporate leadership has become a subject of increasing interest in recent years. Such issues as serious financial scandals in several large companies and increasingly urgent debates about global warming have led to a focus on corporate leadership in general and values-based leadership in particular. It is becoming increasingly apparent that companies must be perceived as having ethical corporate values with respect to social and environmental issues if they are to create a sustainable business. Moreover, these values must be communicated to all stakeholders, and applied effectively throughout the organisation to all corporate strategies, operations, and control systems. This requires values-based corporate leadership.

Leadership is about: (i) understanding and communicating how an organisation can be successful and sustainable; and (ii) giving energy and direction to ensure that this occurs. This chapter focuses on *values-based service leadership* – that is, how leaders develop, communicate, and give practical effect to ethical values that ultimately create value for customers and other stakeholders in producing a sustainable business in the highly competitive global marketplace.

The chapter is structured as follows. First, the chapter explores the concepts of authentic leadership and knowledge sharing in the context of service leadership. Secondly, the chapter describes how IKEA deploys values-based leadership at three levels: the global level, the national level, and the store level. Thirdly, the chapter develops four principles for values-based service leadership. Finally, the chapter discusses what other service companies can learn from IKEA.

Authentic leadership

The concept of 'authentic leadership' has the potential to provide: (i) an effective corrective to the recent increase in management malfeasance; and

(ii) a dynamic leadership model for corporate social responsibility (CSR). The notion of 'authenticity' has been defined by Harter (2002) as:

> ... owning one's personal experiences, be they thoughts, emotions, needs, wants, preferences, or beliefs ... [in accordance with] the injunction to 'know oneself'.

In terms of leadership, such 'authenticity' refers to how leaders live and express their values. Authentic leadership thus reflects what leaders really think and what they really believe in (Ilies *et al.*, 2005). It is *derived from* a leader's self-awareness of his or her fundamental values and purpose; it is *expressed* in consistent behaviours that reflect those values; and its *effect* is to provide motivation to followers who observe the authentic leader's consistent application of values that resonate with their own.

The concept of 'authentic leadership' thus begins with the leader's self-awareness. As Gardner *et al.* (2005, p. 345) observed:

> First and foremost, an authentic leader must achieve [personal] authenticity ... through self-awareness, self-acceptance, and authentic actions and relationships. However, authentic leadership extends beyond the authenticity of the leader as a person to encompass authentic relations with followers and associates. These relationships are characterized by: a) transparency, openness, and trust, b) guidance toward worthy objectives, and c) an emphasis on follower development.

Shamir and Eilam (2005, p. 396) have a similar point of view:

> Authentic leaders are portrayed as possessing self-knowledge and a personal point of view, which reflects clarity about their values and convictions. They are also portrayed as identifying strongly with their leadership role, expressing themselves by enacting that role, and acting on the basis of their values and convictions. Any discussion of authentic leader development has to focus on how these characteristics are developed.

Leading knowledge sharing and transfer

Authentic leaders form an intertwined relationship with their followers (or, in the case of IKEA, with their 'co-workers'). To facilitate the development of such a relationship, IKEA recruits people (both leaders and co-workers) who embrace the IKEA vision and culture. This culture is driven by the corporate values described in the preceding chapters of this book, and authentic leadership is about living these values.

When entering new markets and developing as a globalised company, an ethical firm must maintain (and further develop) these values. To achieve this, *knowledge sharing* and *knowledge transfer* become key competences for a values-based service company. Jonsson (2007, 2008a, 2008b), who analysed the role of multiple knowledge flows when international values-based retail firms (such as IKEA) enter new markets, noted that a new subsidiary must establish itself as a strategic partner to the parent company. According to Jonsson (2008b), three kinds of knowledge flows can be identified in this process: (i) forward knowledge flows; (ii) reverse knowledge flows; and (iii) lateral knowledge flows.

Of these, *forward knowledge flow* is of primary importance because it ensures that the new store in new markets (such as China, Russia, or Japan) is run in a similar way to those in old markets (such as Germany or North America). However, *reverse knowledge flow* is also of importance if an organisation such as IKEA is to understand the special requirements of the new market and how knowledge of these special requirements can be used to benefit the whole company. Finally, *lateral knowledge flow*, which is the sharing of knowledge directly among new markets without going through the centre, is also of value. An example of this in the case of IKEA was a project called the 'Low Purchase Project' (LPP), which involved the sharing of knowledge among IKEA subsidiaries in China, Russia, and Poland with the aim of improving the management of the specific marketing challenges faced in these particular markets (Jonsson, 2008b).

Service leadership

According to Berry (1999, p. 16), service leadership is the engine of service business development:

> Without the energizing vision of leadership, without the direction, the coaching, and the inspiration, the idea of quality improvement is not transformed to action. Great service is a matter of mentality. The quest to improve is unrelenting; ideas are part of the job; the spirit of entrepreneurship is strong. Values guide – not policy and the procedure manuals. Mentality is a matter of leadership ... Nurturing the development of service leadership values and skills is the single most important step an organization can take in the service quality journey. It paves the way for everything else a company might do to improve service.

Berry suggested four ways in which a company can cultivate effective service leadership among its employees: (i) promote the right people; (ii) nurture trust; (iii) emphasise personal involvement; and (iv) encourage leadership learning. In a similar vein, Wirtz *et al.* (2008) addressed the cultivation of effective leadership by developing a model of leadership for service excellence that contained five elements: (i) stringent recruitment and selection processes; (ii) extensive investment in training and re-training; (iii) successful service-delivery teams; (iv) empowerment of frontline staff to control quality; and (v) motivation of staff through rewards and recognition.

Drawing on these suggestions, values-based service leadership is understood in the present book as being: *the motivation and direction of people to create a sustainable service business within the business idea, strategy, and culture of the organisation – resulting in attractive customer value and thus value for other stakeholders.* Viewed in this way, leadership is about creating a vision and formulating clear goals, communicating these goals, and achieving them through prudent utilisation of people and other resources. This requires the creation of trust among leaders, and between leaders and co-workers. Leaders must create an atmosphere that is conducive to people reaching their potential by using their creative energies and skills in developing the business in accordance with the vision, strategy, norms, values, and operational goals enunciated (and enacted) by the leadership.

It is the contention of this book that leaders are made, not born. Leaders grow in an environment in which learning is possible and the career path is clear. Effective leaders create a passion for business development and superior service when the reward systems are clear, fair, and focused on key business development drivers. Authentic leaders have an inner drive motivated by values that are in accordance with the company values. They have the ability to manage people effectively and do not fear conflicts and challenges. They are eager to learn and develop themselves. Most importantly, authentic leaders have a passion to serve their customers and spend time in doing so.

Values-based leadership at three levels in IKEA

IKEA leadership at the global level

Leadership and forward knowledge flows

For a concept-driven retail business such as IKEA, 'forward knowledge flows' are of primary importance. Values-based leadership at the global level requires a dynamic synergy among IKEA's vision, culture, and strategy and a means of ensuring that this synergy promotes a business model that provides the company with a sustainable competitive advantage. In this regard, IKEA's culture fosters innovation and creativity, while viewing mistakes as a natural occurrence in the process of evolution. As the founder and leader of IKEA, Ingvar Kamprad, observed in an article in the *Guardian* (2004): 'Maintaining a strong IKEA culture is one of the most crucial factors behind the continued success of the IKEA concept'.

Kamprad can be said to 'personify' IKEA. His vision, values, and actions have been akin to the role of a 'father' in leading the 'IKEA family'. Management and co-workers alike habitually refer to IKEA using the words 'we' or 'us' (rather than 'it' or 'them'). By adopting this 'paternal' role, Kamprad's vision and leadership style has transformed IKEA into the leading global player in the fragmented industry of furniture retail. His initial vision was (and continues to be) the 'creation of a better everyday life for the majority of people'. This vision was supported by the development of long-term norms and values (such as opposition to child labour), which became incorporated into the IKEA culture to create a sustainable business model. Authentic leaders such as Kamprad communicate a vision, values, and goals in a manner that co-workers can understand and with which they can identify.

In terms of global expansion and the communication of values, co-workers must understand their roles and contributions within the total organisation. In this regard, IKEA relies on the accountability of co-workers and the drive of strong leaders. They want leaders to be 'ambassadors' for the IKEA culture as they consciously develop co-workers (and the business) by acting as role models for others. Training and support are provided to managers to ensure that they have the right skills to encourage and facilitate the development of co-workers in their team (IKEA 2006). Leaders in IKEA emphasise the singular importance of every individual co-worker to ensure that these individuals, in their interactions with customers, can make a real difference.

In a personal interview, Linda Xu (the manager for public relations of IKEA in China) described how Kamprad and Anders Dahlwig (CEO of IKEA) have acted as role models for others in transferring culture and values to employees:

> They provided an example for us. I remember that Ingvar Kamprad, who was more than 70 years of age, sat in economy class when flying to China. Although he is a wealthy man who is famous as the founder of IKEA, he still purchased an economy-class ticket. I was impressed by this behaviour. Similarly, the CEO of IKEA, Anders Dahlvig, flew from Sweden to Guangzhou in China last year; he also travelled economy class ... without any accompanying entourage ... Moreover, the CEO did not have a car (or driver) provided by IKEA. [These examples have

been followed by] the director of IKEA, China, who has no private office. He uses the same office table as I do, and did not have his own secretary until recently

In short, IKEA did not infuse its values and culture through a compulsory structure system. On the contrary, apart from some basic training courses in values and culture, co-workers have absorbed the IKEA culture and corporate values from the role models they see in their everyday work. As a result, these values and culture have become basic to their lives and work.

The IKEA values are thus embedded in the work environment at IKEA and facilitate knowledge sharing across borders. Through the IKEA work environment, co-workers are 'able to contribute to the developments of others' (Jonsson, 2008a, p. 129). Sharing knowledge is part of values-based leadership.

Dahlvig emphasised the importance of leaders personifying the IKEA culture in an interview quoted in Kling and Gateman (2003, p. 35):

There is a connection between the values and the image a person gives. So if you live the values, you also reflect the culture image. Within those values it is also important for all leaders to develop their own style. We don't try to [make] them into a specific type of leader. The framework is our core values, and we allow a lot of freedom depending on who they are and what their specific skills are. I would not ... say that leadership at IKEA is [definitively] A, B, and C ... [rather], leadership for me has to do with motivation. How well my leadership works is reflected in how much I can energize the people. It is about motivation and energy. The relevant question for me is: What is it that really motivates people? I believe the way to motivate people is to make sure they have a clear idea of where they are going and how to contribute to the goal. Having clear goals, a vision, and [a knowledge of] where the business is going – those are the values that are important to me. Building trust in the group that I work with is another important issue. I try to have a very open climate and give a lot of freedom ... What is fundamentally important for us is for people to work well together across functions because they have to understand our pipeline. We have always been good at knowing certain parts, but ... a pipeline-oriented understanding is [now] required. However, we have not been very good at career planning in the past. That is one conscious way of developing people ... I think the biggest challenge comes from ourselves: to see if we can benefit from the advantages of being big and yet not be affected by the disadvantages [that go with it].

Directions for IKEA

Soon after he became CEO in 2001, Dahlvig formulated the directions for IKEA in a document entitled: '10 jobs in 10 years – a direction for IKEA 2001–2010'. This short and easy-to-read document communicated the CEO's leadership directions in implementing the overall business mission, business idea, and company values of IKEA. It included advice on responsibility for suppliers and co-workers, as well as for the environment, in a manner that was relatively uncommon in 2001.

According to the document, one of ten principles was to be the particular focus each year in the subsequent decade. A given principle was thus applied each year to a range of issues – including leadership development, the training of all co-workers, global expansion, the development of the IKEA product range in stores, and the marketing activities of the group.

The ten principles were as follows:

1　To develop a strong and vital range
2　To offer outstanding sales prices
3　To improve our meeting with our customers
4　To continue to reduce purchase prices and improve product quality
5　To develop logistical efficiency in the whole pipeline
6　To attract, develop, and inspire our people
7　To be one IKEA
8　To become leaner, simpler, and quicker
9　To take responsibility for our suppliers, their co-workers, and the environment
10　To keep the culture of IKEA a strong living reality

Leadership and power structure

Organisational structure and power structure are closely linked because both reflect roles and relationships (Johnson *et al.*, 2005). IKEA's conception of leadership at the global level is about creating and maintaining a dynamic power structure in which 'no barriers [exist] between management and co-workers' (IKEA, 2005). The organisation thus rejects a hierarchal structure in opting for informality and open communication lines between leaders and co-workers. IKEA believes that such a 'flat' structure encourages personal development, individual responsibility, and productive collaboration, as well as functioning as an incentive for outstanding performance (Thorvaldsen *et al.*, 2006). Leadership in IKEA is grounded in the total value chain. The production stage creates the prerequisites for a low price, but not at any price. As Kamprad noted in 'The Key' (IKEA, 1995):

We all need to know about production. Knowing how production works has more to do with feelings than with technology. It's about understanding how we need to continue to use new and old techniques and rational manufacturing processes to transform good, inexpensive, and environmentally friendly materials into home furnishings that correspond to the needs and wishes of the majority of people. It's about understanding how, by continuing to make the most rational use of energy and materials, we can reduce our costs and do the planet a favour at the same time. [It's about] realizing the wisdom of always allowing sufficient lead time to be able to acquire materials at the best possible price and plan production to run smoothly.

Leadership and recruitment

Qualities apart from education and skills are counted as important in the IKEA recruitment process. IKEA recruits employees who share IKEA values. Moreover, the company wants to attract people of diverse nationalities with a variety of perspectives and experiences. According to IKEA (2006), such diversity makes IKEA a better place in which to work and shop.

Recruiting the right people is vital for the company's growth and expansion into international markets. An IKEA manager in Sweden made the following observations about recruitment (Jonsson, 2008a):

IKEA is very much driven by development. We talk about growth ... and we do need to grow as a company. But to do so we need 'growing people'. It starts with recruitment – having people who are willing to take risks. The people whom we want to stay with us accept the challenges of the job and want to grow. We do not need to pay high salaries and provide other benefits. Rather, we promise that we will grow and expand with the people we recruit.

Anti-bureaucratic week

IKEA organises an annual 'anti-bureaucratic week', during which all leaders are expected to take part in 'hands-on' working activities with customers and co-workers in a store, showroom, or warehouse. According to the CEO of IKEA, '... this is the way we stay close to reality and focused on what is most important for our customers'.

Even the IKEA Group President, Anders Dahlvig, has taken part in 'anti-bureaucratic week'. In 2006 he worked at the IKEA store in Stockholm for several days, wearing a badge saying: 'I'm new to IKEA'. Dahlvig saw IKEA from a different perspective as he replenished stock, worked in self-serve, and sold beds. 'He did a great job and was eager to learn,' reported Anna Karlsson, who took care of him. 'He was particularly interested in our packaging and how it could be improved. But I hardly gave a thought to the fact that he was Group President.' Although Dahlvig has now returned to his own work, the legacy of his work experience lives on. 'It was very thought-provoking,' he said. 'I learnt a lot about our range – about what works and what doesn't.'

In a similar vein, the president of IKEA Sweden, Jeanette Söderberg, spends one day every month meeting customers and co-workers in various IKEA stores in Sweden to ensure that she remains in touch with 'reality'.

IKEA leadership at the national level

The business model of the IKEA concept at the global level is implemented at the national level in every country. In each country in which it has one or more stores, IKEA has a national leader. There is also a service office (SO) supporting the stores with a national sales manager, human-resources manager, marketing manager, and financial manager.

IKEA Sweden

Leadership at the national level can best be exemplified by the situation in Sweden, the country in which IKEA began. The national president in Sweden is Jeanette Söderberg, who began working with IKEA in 1983. After ten years with IKEA, she was recruited to leadership positions outside the firm, but returned as a store manager in 2003 before becoming national president for Sweden in 2005. As national president for Sweden, Söderberg reports to the president of IKEA Europe.

IKEA Sweden has 17 stores in 2008, of which 16 are owned by IKEA and one is franchised. The managers of these stores report to the president at the national level. However, store managers are expected to develop their own strategies and business goals on the basis of their analysis of the local market conditions.

The main task for a national president is to maximise IKEA's business potential in that country. The role involves the implementation of IKEA's global strategies while simultaneously questioning what is done and why. The national president is expected to create an entrepreneurial culture, formulate challenging business goals for all leaders, delegate responsibility (in combination with support), and control all systems and activities. According to the national president for Sweden, it is important to have 'a passion for the vision'. A recent study among IKEA co-workers in Sweden showed that 95 per cent of respondents knew the vision and the business goals of the organisation and that 80 per cent stated that they were inspired by them.

Four areas of national leadership can be emphasised:

- *Business goals:* Challenging business goals must be formulated, along with effective strategies to achieve those goals.
- *Values-based leadership:* Leaders must be role models and they must meet and relate to the customer at all levels in the organisation. For one day in every month, Söderberg puts on the IKEA uniform and works in an IKEA store to meet and converse with customers and co-workers. National leaders must be directed by IKEA's values while always questioning what is being done and how it is being done. They do follow routines, checklists, and manuals, but they always ensure that they are easy to use and an effective means of reaching business goals.
- *Focus on the individual:* It is important for a national leader to create opportunities for managers and co-workers, to provide energy, and to give direction, while simultaneously encouraging responsibility and freedom.
- *Focus on the task:* It is important for a national leader to focus on tasks that are within his or her capacity to control, and to ensure that these tasks are seen through to the end.

In its formal structure, IKEA Sweden has a board of directors that is chaired by the president for IKEA Europe. The national president for IKEA Sweden is supported by an executive team that includes a vice-president, together with managers for marketing, sales, logistics, finance, human resources, and public relations and communication.

The national president has a complex role in relating to senior management at the regional and global levels of IKEA, as well as relating to managers and co-workers at the local (store) level and to other companies within the IKEA group. Although this complexity implies many challenges for the national leaders, the IKEA culture facilitates collaborative relationships through its emphasis on humility and respect for different roles, competencies, and responsibilities. This encourages open questioning and frank discussions at meetings at all levels.

The role of national leader also includes the development of future leaders. All potential leaders are assessed and 'mapped' in a systematic manner on the basis of their individual performance. The emphasis is on helping co-workers and leaders to grow as individuals, and thus contribute to the development of IKEA.

IKEA US

To become successful in the United States, IKEA was forced to make changes to the concept that had previously worked well in Asia and Europe. IKEA had entered the American market in 1985; however, after two years, sales began to decrease alarmingly. It was apparent that certain aspects of the IKEA concept were not understood or appreciated by Americans. To adjust to American culture, it was necessary for IKEA to undertake significant changes in the concept. At the time this was a new experience for IKEA, but the company has subsequently been forced to undertake appropriate cultural adjustments in other countries as well. Although the essential structure of the IKEA idea remained untouched, some 'fine-tuning' was required to 'Americanise' the concept. As a result of these changes, penetration of the US market improved significantly.

IKEA now has ambitions to grow in the US. According to Pernille Lopez, the national leader of IKEA US, IKEA is on a mission to become the leading home-furnishing company in the United States. By 2008, IKEA had 34 stores in the US and had plans to open 3–5 new stores every year in future. This expansion represents a challenge for the leadership. To help meet this challenge, a booklet entitled 'Growth' (IKEA US, 2005) provides inspirational guidance for the IKEA leadership in the United States from the national president. The nature of the messages in this inspirational policy document can be gauged from the excerpt in the box.

To support growth in the United States, IKEA has built a new service centre that also serves as the headquarters for IKEA US. The new building, which is situated in Philadelphia, is a workplace for 350 co-workers and is certified by 'Leadership in Energy and Environmental Design' (LEED) as a building that does not have an adverse effect on the environment.

The service centre is situated adjacent to an IKEA store. A member of the IKEA US executive team commented on the significance of this in the following terms:

> It is good for the service centre to be so close to our customers. When we have project meetings we take … the opportunity to walk through the store and stop in specific areas where we are creating new solutions. In this way we are always close to the reality of the customers.

Recruiting co-workers at national level for the global expansion

IKEA recruits 20,000 new employees per year. All of these new co-workers are recruited at the national level, although many transfer between various countries. IKEA believes that diversity creates a more challenging business

---

Growth

We are growing fast. We have big plans. Our mission is to be the leading home furnishing company [in the US]. And so we have set clear goals to help us all focus on the work ahead. You are part of this. We need your spirit, your passion, your drive, and your desire to succeed. As you read this, ask yourself: 'Where do I fit in? What else needs to be done? What ideas do I have that can help?

Develop and inspire each other ... Do well what you do now. Competence breeds confidence. Be a strong leader. Ask 'why?' and 'why not?' Take time to learn your job. Don't say no ... trust more. Listen better. Be clear. Make feedback count. Teach, wonder, learn, and make tough decisions. Lead by example. Run with the ball, ask for help, and expect the unexpected. Forge a new path, find common ground, erase barriers. Open yourself up to new ideas, to others, [and] to the future ... Lead by example, stay humble, respect yourself and others. ... It's more than a job, it's a way of life.

Adapted from 'Growth' (IKEA US, 2005)

---

atmosphere and expands the recruitment base. They then receive training in meeting IKEA's customers in accordance with the firm's values and with an appropriate level of competence.

IKEA leadership at the store level

Leaders and co-workers in the front line at the store level know the local language, customs and values of their customers. This is facilitated by the fact that most of the leaders in local stores began their working lives in the store in which they now work as they pursued their career paths within IKEA.

Kuala Lumpur (Malaysia)

The manager of the IKEA store in Kuala Lumpur, Åsa Hjort, noted in an interview in 2003 that the most significant cultural difference between Malaysia and IKEA is the non-hierarchical structure and style of IKEA's leadership. Many companies in Malaysia can be described as 'hierarchical', and employees coming from such organisations can experience difficulties in understanding and adjusting to the way in which IKEA is managed. As Hjort observed in the interview:

> You need to be very clear when it comes to what has been agreed on and when it is to be done. The culture in Malaysia is much different from Sweden ... I sometimes ask staff to repeat what we have decided to do to make sure there is no misunderstanding.

The recruitment of appropriate staff at the store level is a cornerstone of IKEA practice, and this is of particular importance in Malaysia. This involves: (i) formal personality tests for all potential recruits; (ii) detailed scanning of educational and work experiences; and (iii) personal interviews (in which senior management is involved). A service-oriented attitude and experience of retailing are the two most important criteria when selecting and recruiting leaders and co-workers. If potential recruits lack specific skills, IKEA adopts the attitude that this can be easily rectified by organising specific training in particular areas.

Singapore

In an interview in December 2003, Terrence Nielsen, the IKEA store manager in Singapore, was asked about the most important success factors for an IKEA store in Singapore. Nielsen emphasised the creation of positive memorable experiences through: (i) the key role of the IKEA culture; (ii) a service orientation among co-workers (in terms of attitude and behaviour in interaction with customers); and (iii) well-designed, functional, and low-priced furniture. Nielsen also emphasised the importance of children: 'They are our future customers, and if they are happy the parents will be happy, stay longer in the store, and buy more'.

Karlstad (Sweden)

In an interview with the present authors in 2007, Susanne Jensert, the IKEA store manager in Karlstad (Sweden), described the important roles played by the IKEA culture, the business model, and the 'IKEA Way' in directing operations when establishing a new store:

> IKEA has a matrix organization with various IKEA companies being responsible for the real estate, the products and the assortment, product development, the IKEA brand, and so on. We have a national manager and each of my function-leaders in the executive team in the store has someone at the national level from whom they receive advice and

direction. We do make decisions at the store level, but ... we have clear roles, guidelines, and systems at the national and global levels. There is dialogue, within various areas, between the leaders at the national level and the leaders at the store level ... The strategic and long-term decisions are taken at the corporate level and have implications for IKEA globally. It is clear that the vision and business strategy at the corporate level have major implications for how we manage at the store level. We always focus on how to best serve our customers and at the same time create a working environment that is attractive and supportive of the co-workers.

When we recruit leaders and co-workers, it is most important that they share our values ... we focus on three factors: First, competence in retailing in general and in ... the specific tasks to be carried out. Secondly, leadership experience from retailing or other related organisations. Thirdly, the values [of IKEA], which are always most important ... We try to adapt the training programs to each individual co-worker's needs, depending on previous experiences ... and specific needs. Before they start work, the leaders have 2–4 weeks of training – both practical training (working at other stores) and more theoretical training (in relevant areas of the store). The co-workers have at least two weeks of training when they start working.

I have total responsibility for the business aspects of the store. I have an executive team of six persons (including me). They cover such areas as finance and management control, sales, logistics, customer relationships, and ... human resources. We have a clear focus on making it easy and attractive for customers to visit the store. We have a Småland [play area] for the children and 'IKEA Family' [customer club] to manage the relationships with our most loyal customers. We also emphasise environmental issues with the co-workers. IKEA must be an attractive employer, and we have a development plan for each co-worker and leader. We have at least one co-worker appraisal per year.

Funabashi (Japan)

Jonsson (2007) observed knowledge sharing at the 'micro level' at the IKEA store in Funabashi (Japan). The focus of the study was on how the store manager and her co-workers interacted with one another on the store floor and how they interacted with the wider IKEA network. Utilising Nonaka's (1994) model of *socialization, externalization, combination,* and *internalization*, Jonsson (2007, pp. 335–6) came to the following conclusions:

The observations illustrate that a micro-level internalization is the most common mode for knowledge sharing. This makes sense as the co-workers preferred to search for their own and new solutions, rather than consulting best practices found in manuals or on the Intranet. Socialization was also evident where new co-workers worked as apprentices and where employee rotation was encouraged. Externalization and combination were less evident. The reason for this was that not all co-workers knew where to find relevant information or how to interpret it. It was stressed that if you do not have the right IKEA knowledge you will not be able to interpret the enormous amount of data available in manuals and on Intranet. Another reason might be that externalization and combination relates more to issues related to a macro perspective – i.e. tools and mechanisms controlled at management level.

It was thus apparent that the management team at the store level provides a link between those who undertake their daily tasks within the store and the wider IKEA network outside the store.

Conclusions regarding leadership at the store level

IKEA leadership at the store level displays the cultural characteristics described by Brown (1998), who suggested that a strong leadership culture leads to exceptional performance through goal alignment, employee motivation, and an ability to learn from the past. Co-workers at IKEA tend to agree on what goals to pursue and how to achieve those goals. Their enthusiasm and initiative are focused in accordance with a strong sense of shared motivational values. In addition, norms of behaviour, stories, and rituals are used to reinforce co-workers' interpretations of events, which promote understanding, social cohesion, and consensus in meeting new challenges. As Thorvaldsen *et al.* (2006) noted, IKEA co-workers are bombarded with elements of the IKEA culture from their first day on the job; they are aware of what the company stands for and they develop the behavioural norms that are expected of them.

Four principles for values-based service leadership

Four principles of values-based service leadership for sustainable business can be derived from a review of the pertinent literature and the studies of the IKEA leadership described above. The four principles are:

- live the company values to create customer value;

- promote the right people;
- trust employees and customers and emphasise their involvement; and
- reward learning and innovation.

Each of these is described in more detail below.

Live the company values to create customer value

The leadership of any organisation must 'live' its corporate culture as role models of the assumptions, behaviours, and routines of the organisation that are otherwise 'taken for granted' (Johnson *et al.*, 2005). In so doing, the underlying values of the organisation are expressed through the actions and behaviour of leaders; not merely what they say, but what they do and how they do it.

The essential notion of 'belonging to a family' was emphasised decades ago when IKEA began, and it remains a cornerstone of the now globalised company. This notion of 'family' extends beyond the leaders and co-workers of the organisation to include its loyal customers. As Kamprad observed:

> Once and for all we have decided to side with the many. What is good for our customers is also good for us in the long run. This is an objective that entails responsibility.

Promote the right people

The overwhelming majority of IKEA leaders are identified, developed, and promoted from within the organisation. The best way to nurture service leadership is to recruit and promote people on the basis of criteria that are firmly grounded in service excellence. Such people are more likely to act as service-minded and customer-centric role models for others in the organisation. They show their co-workers how to create results, in both the long term and the short term, through their own attitudes and behaviour. Modelling leaders' behaviours is a particularly powerful way of cultivating leadership values and skills. As Berry (1999, p. 17) observed: 'Placing a true leader in charge helps to transform followers into leaders themselves'.

Berry (1999) suggested five questions that should be posed in recruiting and promoting the right people:

1   What are the person's greatest career accomplishments (and why)?
2   What innovations or new directions did this person sponsor in previous positions?

3   What is this person's philosophy of service? What evidence suggests that this individual will be a service leader?
4   Does this person inspire others and build fellowship? Do others believe in this individual? Do they believe in his or her integrity?
5   Is there evidence of informal leadership in this person's background; that is, the ability to influence a group without the benefit of an official position or title?

These five questions suggest that a basic 'leadership test' is the extent to which a person's values and priorities are apparent for all to see. The 'footprint-in-the sand', as Berry (1999) described it, can provide companies with valuable insights into a person's leadership potential.

Trust employees and customers and emphasise their involvement

According to Berry (1999, p. 19):

> Personal involvement in service improvement builds insight, fosters commitment, and stimulates leadership. When people in organizations are invited to participate in service improvement, to become genuine partners in an endeavor as challenging, sensible, and potentially gratifying as service excellence, many will give their ideas, energy, and spirit to the cause.

Good leaders know how to trust people. Trust is the prerequisite for openness, creativity, and involvement. Trust is built from the top, and then permeates throughout the organisation through authentic leadership; if leaders trust their co-workers, they will, in turn, trust their customers. And, in most cases, the customers will then respond with loyalty to the firm.

Personal involvement with IKEA is emphasised at every level of the organisation. Leaders and co-workers are expected to identify with the company, its products, and its service to customers. To encourage such personal involvement throughout the organisation, leaders must spend time with customers and co-workers, and demonstrate their trust in them. Trust inspires a sense of 'ownership' in the business and inspires leadership behaviour among co-workers. People who feel that they are trusted 'owners' of the IKEA values want to improve the business and work harder.

Trust implies reliance on co-workers and customers. Authentic leaders assume that employees and customers are essentially honest; for example, they do not adopt a suspicious or cynical attitude as they listen to complaining customers relating their grievances. Moreover, such trusting responsibility is delegated to front-line IKEA co-workers, who are trained and empowered to make decisions themselves when complaining customers describe their problems. For example, a customer might complain that some screws were missing from the pack when they purchased a piece of furniture. Frontline employees never ask: 'Are you sure that you have not misplaced the screws?' Such a question would imply a lack of trust in the customer. Rather, co-workers are trained to respond: 'I am sorry, how many screws do you need?' The IKEA policy is that customers must always be trusted – unless the co-worker has indisputable evidence that the customer is attempting to take unfair advantage.

Reward learning and innovation

According to Berry (1999, p. 27):

> Service leadership values and skills can be learned. Companies aspiring to excellent service should be prepared to invest in leadership learning on a continuous basis and on multiple fronts.

One way of identifying and nurturing leadership skills is to place staff members in situations that are new to them and in which their existing skills, experiences, and knowledge are insufficient to resolve the situation. In such situations, leadership potential might emerge as it becomes apparent that the 'old ways' of doing things are insufficient and that there are no 'safe' solutions. Such 'challenge learning' is often used in IKEA to stimulate reverse knowledge flows and lateral knowledge flows as new 'smart' solutions emerge at the local level and influence the global concept.

In accordance with the guiding principle of seeking 'a better life for the many', IKEA leaders are encouraged to focus on solving the real-life problems of customers at home. IKEA leaders therefore spend time with customers and co-workers listening to their views, disappointments, and suggestions. Indeed, the founder and owner of IKEA, Ingvar Kamprad, visits 25–30 IKEA stores every year meeting customers and co-workers. A particular focus of his discussions is the exposure of IKEA products to customers, and innovative ways of ensuring that customers can experience IKEA solutions to their real-life problems at home. As Kamprad (IKEA 2007a) explained: 'The customer must be able to see, feel, and be interested in our products'.

Innovative solutions to real-life problems at home require a combination of form, function, and low price. The idea of 'lean production' has always been a key issue in IKEA, not only for environmental reasons but also to enable the company to offer well-designed, functional furniture that is affordable for the majority of people. Innovative solutions can involve a small detail – such as an improvement in the packaging of screws to make it easier for customers to assemble a piece of furniture. Other innovative solutions can involve larger projects – such as the development of the 'IKEA Family' (the customer club) in the early 1980s. New ideas and innovative solutions are encouraged, recognised, and rewarded.

Implications for other companies

Compare and learn but not copy

The IKEA leadership model is clearly grounded in a strong culture that forms the basis for the IKEA way of doing business. Other companies can learn from this by creating a clear business model, applying it in all parts of the organisation, and ensuring that it is dynamic through knowledge sharing. Such a dynamic business model is capable of appropriate adjustment over time if authentic leaders remain close to the customers and the key processes of the total value chain.

This requires development strategies that are planned and enacted at the *global level*, supported and nurtured at the *national level*, and sensitively managed in terms of local requirements at the *store level*. Moreover, it must be applied to all business functions – including purchasing, logistics, information technology, financial control, building new stores, and a customer club.

Create a strong culture and a clear business model

Creating a strong values-based culture requires a continuous learning processes (Post *et al.*, 2002) led by authentic leadership and knowledge sharing. However, the values that underlie the culture have to be authentically rooted in the history and mission of the organisation.

A clear business model can then emerge from these values-based ideas as practical guidelines, manuals, and Intranet support are developed. The business model is thus built on shared values in the company with a view to a 'triple bottom line' (economic, social, and environmental) assessment of the co-creation of value-in-use with customers and other stakeholders.

Service innovation as co-creation of value

The focus within IKEA is clearly on serving customers by providing solutions to real-life problems at home. The IKEA culture is avowedly customer-centric while maintaining a clear focus on corporate social responsibility, environmental responsibility, lean production, and cost-consciousness. Within this framework, service innovations are derived not only from forward knowledge flows, but also from reverse and lateral knowledge flows as they emerge from interactions with co-workers, suppliers, and customers.

This understanding of service innovation rests on the premise that 'service' is best understood as an exercise in value creation in which customers play an essential role as co-creators and co-producers. Such an understanding of service innovation (and the role of customers as co-creators and co-producers) can be applied to any organisation in any industry. But to apply this conception of service innovation successfully, leaders must remain close to their customers and their employees. Companies need to understand what drives customer value, and then focus their leadership on these drivers with a view to differentiating themselves from other companies in their particular industry.

Leadership development as a systematic and planned process

Leadership development should not be seen as a separate activity, but as an integral aspect of a dynamic, values-based business model. Leadership is about creating energy and motivation for employees to provide superior service for customers in reaching business goals. Systematically planned leadership programmes and employee training schemes can ensure that the corporate culture is transmitted to all levels of the organisation.

Leadership development is a real challenge for an expanding business. Decisions regarding the recruitment of new employees and leaders have long-term consequences, and such decisions are therefore among the most important that an organisation can make. As noted above, IKEA has made a conscious decision to recruit co-workers and first-line managers locally – to ensure that the firm is represented by people who know the language and culture in which IKEA is functioning. IKEA utilises clear and known criteria in making decisions about recruitment, rewards, and promotion. Leaders in the middle and upper levels of management are provided with mentors who support and assess their accomplishments. In all of this, IKEA recognises the seminal importance of how co-workers are treated and leaders are developed.

Questions

1   What leadership qualities are rewarded in your organisation (and why)?
2   How much time do the leaders of your organisation spend with customers and employees?

3   What values are communicated as being the most important (and how are they communicated)?
4   Does quality of leadership have implications for service excellence?
5   How is leadership learning encouraged and rewarded in your organisation?
6   How is leadership change planned and managed?
7   Do leaders in your organisation trust employees and customers?
8   What can you learn from values-based leadership from IKEA? How can you apply this in your organisation?

References

Berry, L. (1999) *On Great Service*. New York: Free Press.

Brown, A. (1998) *Organisational Culture*, 2nd edition. Harlow: Prentice Hall.

Gardner, W.L., Avolio, B.J., Luthans, F., May, D.R. and Walumbwa, F. (2005) Can you see the real me? A self-based model of authentic leader and follower development, *The Leadership Quarterly*, Vol. 16, No. 3, pp. 343–72.

Guardian (June 2004) The miracle of Älmhult. [Internet]. Available from: http://www.guardian.co.uk/g2/story/0,3604,1240462,00.html.

Harter, S. (2002) Authenticity, in C.R. Snyder and S. Lopez (eds), *Handbook of Positive Psychology*. Oxford: Oxford University Press.

IKEA (1995) *The Key*, Inter IKEA Systems.

IKEA (2005) Social and Environmental Responsibility report.

IKEA (2006) Social and Environmental Responsibility report.

IKEA (2007a) *Interview with Ingvar Kamprad*, IKEA Family Live, February 2007.

IKEA (2007b) IKEA corporate website. [Internet].

IKEA US (2005) *Growth*. Internal strategy document. IKEA United States.

IKEA US (2007) *Home Welcome Home* (Booklet about IKEA North America Services new office building).

Ilies, R., Morgeson, F.P. and Nahrgang, J.D. (2005) Authentic leadership and eudaemonic well-being: Understanding leader–follower outcomes, *The Leaderaship Quaterly*, Vol. 16, No. 3, pp. 373–94.

Johnson, G., Scholes, K. and Whittington, R. (2005) *Exploring Corporate Strategy – Text and Cases*, 7th edition. Harlow: Prentice Hall.

Jonsson, A. (2007) *Knowledge Sharing at Micro Level: A Participant Observation at IKEA Japan*. The Institute of Economic Research Working Paper Series, 2007:2, Lund University.

Jonsson, A. (2008a) *Knowledge Sharing Across Borders – A Study in the IKEA World*, Lund Business Press, Lund Studies in Economics and Management 97.

Jonsson, A. (2008b) A Transnational Perspective on Knowledge sharing: Lessons from IKEA's Entry into Russia, China and Japan, *The International Review of Retail, Distribution and Consumer Research*, Vol. 18, No. 1, pp. 17–44.

Kling, K. and Gateman, I. (2003) IKEA CEO Anders Dahlvig on international growth and IKEA's unique corporate culture and brand identity, *Academy of Management Executive*, Vol. 17, No. 1, pp. 31–7.

Kouzes, J.M. and Barry, Z. (1995) *The Leadership Challenge*. New York: Jossey-Bass.

Mintel (2004) Furniture Retail – UK – August 2004 [Internet], Available from: http://reports.mintel.com/mintel/searchexec/.

Nonaka, I. (1994) A dynamic theory of organizational knowledge creation, *Organization Science*, Vol. 5, No. 1, pp. 14–37.

Normann, R. (2001) *Reframing Business – When the Map Changes the Landscape*. Chichester: Wiley.

Normann, R. and Ramirez, R. (1993) From value chain to value constellation: designing interactive strategy, *Harvard Business Review*, Vol. 46, July–August, pp. 65–77.

Post, J.E., Preston, L.E. and Sachs, S. (2002) *Redefining the Corporation – Stakeholder Management and Organizational Wealth*. Los Angeles, CA: Stanford University Press.

Schein, E. (1992) *Organizational Culture and Leadership*. San Francisco, CA: Jossey-Bass.

Shamir, B. and Eilam, G. (2005) What's your story? A life-stories approach to authentic leadership development, *The Leadership Quarterly*, Vol. 16, No. 3, pp. 395–417.

Thorvaldsen, M., Mulvana, K., Kawalewale, J., Trosterud, T.A. and Evans. J. (2006) Critically examine how the success of IKEA has been supported by its organizational culture. Unpublished working paper, Leeds Business School.

Torekull, B. (1999) *Leading by Design*. New York: Harper Business.

Wirtz, J., Heracleous, L. and Pangarkar, N. (2008) Managing human resources for service excellence and cost effectiveness at Singapore Airlines, *Managing Service Quality*, Vol. 18, No. 1, pp. 4–19.

7 Values-based sustainable service business

Introduction

This chapter begins with a summary of the lessons that can be learnt from IKEA in Chapters 1–6, followed by a comparison with other values-based firms (Starbucks, H&M, and Body Shop). Based on this comparison, the chapter then proposes several principles for successful values-based service businesses and illustrates these principles with examples from the studied companies. Finally, the chapter concludes by presenting a model for a values-based service business.

Lessons from IKEA

The lessons to be learnt from this book's study of IKEA can be summarised in five areas as follows: (i) a new entrepreneurial business model; (ii) the logic of values and the logic of value creation; (iii) service experience; (iv) service brand and marketing communication; and (v) service leadership.

A new entrepreneurial business model

As noted in earlier chapters, IKEA began in a poor farm village in the southern Swedish county of Småland. The entrepreneur, Ingvar Kamprad, challenged established views from the beginning. For example, he believed that an entrepreneur should first make money before spending or investing; he disliked being dependent on loans from a bank.

IKEA's original focus was on furniture that had 'function', 'quality', and 'low price', and these attributes (together with the later addition of 'good design') remain the core components of the business model that is firmly embedded in the IKEA culture. The original supply chain and business model of IKEA had to cope with the limited resources that existed in the relatively poor district of Småland, but this lack of resources had the virtue of stimulating the creation of 'smart' solutions. In summing-up his entrepreneurial vision, Kamprad observed: 'The question is whether, as an entrepreneur, I [could] combine the good in a profit-making business with a lasting human social vision. I like to think that it must be possible.'

In focusing on smart solutions, Kamprad created the concept of furniture that customers could put together themselves. This resulted in lower warehouse and distribution costs, but it did require new ways of producing the products and new packaging (with instructions to the customers on how to assemble it). In effect, the customers became 'co-producers' of the IKEA solutions as some of the activities were transferred to the customers. This is the core of the IKEA business model, which has been further developed by a sophisticated supply chain and a systematic renewal of products and service offerings.

In addition, the marketing activities of IKEA, which used creative themes and emphasised the development of the IKEA brand, challenged established views of marketing in the industry. Moreover, the business model now also includes the establishment of new stores and the requisite transfer of IKEA knowledge and values from established markets to new markets in a variety of national cultures.

The culture in IKEA is based on shared values and meanings. The IKEA values are: (i) togetherness and enthusiasm; (ii) constant desire for renewal; (iii) cost consciousness; (iv) willingness to accept and delegate responsibility; (v) humbleness and willpower; (vi) simplicity; (vii) leadership by example; (viii) daring to be different; (ix) striving to meet reality; (x) constantly being 'on the way'; and (xi) being unafraid of making mistakes (with the privilege of making mistakes and putting them right afterwards).

These values drive the company's strategy and provide guidance to leaders and co-workers alike. The values thus provide motivation to maximise the commercial potential of the company at all levels. The underlying theme is a customer focus (as IKEA puts it, 'to stand by the many'), combined with social and environmental responsibility. The focus is on solutions to real-life problems at home for the majority of people.

IKEA emphasises corporate social responsibility (CSR). IKEA's long-term strategy is to create a better life for all stakeholders. In this regard, social and environmental responsibility is a natural part of the IKEA business model. According to IKEA, social and environmental responsibility is profitable in the long run and is in accordance with IKEA's commitment to being cost-conscious.

Apart from the values held by its leaders and co-workers, the IKEA service strategy is driven by external pressure from customers, non-government organisations (NGOs), and competitors. The success of IKEA is based on the conviction that values and meanings are co-created among all members of the IKEA stakeholder network in various market contexts.

The logic of values and the logic of value

According to the traditional view, value is defined and created in the value chain and incorporated into products during product development and production. In contrast, the emerging view, as adopted by IKEA, is that value is co-created with customers and assessed on the basis of value-in-use during consumption experiences. In adopting this view, IKEA promotes its furniture and other products as 'enablers' of smart solutions to real-life problems at home. These solutions are co-created with the customer and their value is primarily assessed when the products are used. Value is thus predominantly assessed in terms of *value-in-use*.

This conception of the *logic of value* (whereby customers assess quality in terms of how design and function provide solutions to problems) is combined at IKEA with a *logic of values* (whereby special attention is paid to the ethical, social, and environmental values that are increasingly playing a prominent role in customers' decisions to buy). Consumers have an increasing awareness of environmental, social, and ethical issues, which has resulted in corporate social responsibility (CSR) becoming a driving force in business development. IKEA's commitment to CSR is part of its wider commitment to its various stakeholders (including customers. co-workers, and suppliers). The social and environmental policies of IKEA are rooted in the core values of the company.

Service experience

Apart from value-in-use after the purchase, IKEA also creates value for its customers through the co-creation of individualised solutions during pre-purchase service experiences. This simultaneously reduces risk for the customer and enhances customer imagination and interaction with the organisation.

So called 'hyperreality' is also used to provide customers with a pre-purchase service experiences. Just as product-based organisations have traditionally allowed their customers to 'test-drive' their products, service organisations are increasingly utilising simulated or 'hyperreal' services to enable customers to experience potential service solutions before purchase. In the case of IKEA, the firm enables customers to experience a new kitchen in the store and/or to use web-based experiences (such as the IKEA 'kitchen planner') to simulate or 'test-drive' customized solutions.

An 'experience room' can support customers in their role as co-creators of value (make the solutions customised and 'tangible'), as well as facilitating the company's communication of its corporate values. In this regard, the IKEA showrooms can be seen as 'experience rooms', in which customers receive a 'real' service experience before purchase.

Service brand and marketing communication

Three essential elements – vision, culture, and image – must be aligned if a values-based brand strategy is to be successful. In IKEA's marketing, value-in-use for customers is primarily of an instrumental nature, as communicated through the catalogue, the website, and the store showrooms. However, in IKEA's marketing strategy there is also communication beyond the instrumental level, whereby IKEA narrates a sustainable corporate 'story' in which vision, culture, and image complement one another in a successful branding strategy.

Taken together, IKEA's vision, business idea, and market positioning provide a framework for brand-building that is used in the entire firm's marketing communication worldwide. The brand embodies and expresses values that add value when customers experience solutions to real-life problems at home.

To ensure sustainable success, a company needs to focus on a few basic values that are attractive to customers, employees, and other stakeholders. In particular, it is essential that the company's values and those of the customers achieve so-called 'values resonance'. The IKEA brand is built on associations with such values as cost-consciousness, design, unconventionality, and environmental awareness.

IKEA recognises the importance of training, empowering, and rewarding leaders and co-workers to 'live the brand' in their interactions with one another, customers, suppliers, other partners, the media, and owners. 'Living the IKEA brand' is learnt by co-workers and leaders in their day-to-day work, in on-the-job training, and through educational programmes that explain the IKEA way.

Service leadership

IKEA has created a strong culture built on authentic leadership and knowledge sharing. Most IKEA leaders are identified, developed, and promoted from within the organisation. Within the IKEA network, the values and skills of the organisation are cultivated by shared knowledge and authentic leadership. Leaders are promoted on the basis of their personal values, skills, potential, and what they have delivered so far. The sharing of

IKEA values among leaders and co-workers ensures that values resonance within the firm provides energy and direction for sustainable business development.

IKEA trusts its leaders, co-workers, and customers, and emphasises the importance of their involvement. Trust is a pre-requisite for openness, creativity, and involvement. It is built from the top through authentic leadership, involvement, responsibility, and empowerment. In IKEA's view, when co-workers and leaders grow, the business is growing. In the IKEA network, reverse knowledge flows and lateral knowledge flows ensure that new smart solutions become a reality and have an influence on the global concept.

Comparison with other values-based service companies

It is interesting to compare IKEA with three other well-known values-based service companies – Starbucks, H&M, and Body Shop – all of which are recognised as role models in their industries.

Starbucks

Starbucks Coffee Company opened its first coffee retail store in Seattle (United States) in 1971. The Starbucks Corporation was formed in 1985, with its founder, Howard Schultz, as CEO at that time in the company.

The mission of Starbucks is: 'To establish Starbucks as the premier purveyor of the finest coffees in the world while maintaining its uncompromising principles as we grow'. The six guiding principles of the company are:

- To provide a great work environment and treat each other with respect and dignity.
- To embrace diversity as an essential component of the way we do business.
- To apply the highest standards of excellence to the purchasing, roasting, and fresh delivery of our coffee.
- To develop enthusiastically satisfied customers all of the time.
- To contribute positively to our communities and our environment.
- To recognise that profitability is essential to our future success.

Starbucks is listed on the stock market, and the employees (who are referred to as 'partners') have always been offered an opportunity to buy shares in the company.

Starbucks has become the world's leading retailer, roaster, and brand of specialty coffee with coffee houses around the world. The Starbucks brand is known for customer satisfaction, consistently high-quality products, and a relaxed and inviting atmosphere in its coffee houses (Michelli, 2007). Starbucks is a member of UN Global Compact, and its service culture is based on 'triple bottom line' (TBL) thinking and good citizenship.

The firm aims to control its supply chain – from farmers to retailers – in an ethical manner. To achieve this, the firm has instituted a stringent set of regulations and criteria for choosing farmers, processors, exporters, importers, distributors, and retailers. Starbucks is a company with a strong commitment to all its stakeholders – including customers, shareholders, employees, suppliers, strategic partners, local communities, and global society.

According to Michelli (2007):

> The genius of Starbucks' success lies in its ability to create personalized customer experiences, stimulate business growth, generate profits, energize employees, and secure customer loyalty – all at the same time … Exploring the long-term well-being of partners and those individuals whose lives the partners touch, all the while being mindful of the earth's ability to sustain the demands that Starbucks places on it. Specifically, it means things like Starbucks' exploration of alternative and renewable energy options.

H&M

H&M (formerly 'Hennes & Mauritz') is a growing Swedish clothing retailer with approximately 1,400 stores in 28 countries, including Europe, the USA, and East Asia. H&M is a member of the UN Global Compact, and its service culture is based on TBL thinking. The company communicates its responsibilities as a corporate citizen to all its stakeholders and members of the supply chain.

H&M is listed on the stock market. The chairman and major shareholder is Stefan Persson, who is the son of the entrepreneurial founder of the company. This lineage has helped the company to retain the founding family's sense of responsibility towards its customers and the environment.

H&M is a values-based company with a strong commitment to all its stakeholders – including shareholders, customers, employees (who are referred to as 'colleagues'), suppliers, and strategic partners. H&M ensures that its products are of good quality through continuous quality controls, and aims to produce the items with minimal impact on the environment and under good working conditions. H&M has its own codes of conduct.

For example, H&M has implemented controls on chemical hazards in advance of legislative requirements. The company has a focus on customer value and encourages its designers, product-development staff, and quality staff to work closely with suppliers to learn about materials selection, manufacturing, and quality. The company's focus on the total supply chain and quality improvements characterises its CSR activities. The company keeps its prices low through efficient management of production and logistics.

H&M's innovative concept is to design, produce, and distribute clothes at a price that is accessible to the majority of people. H&M was a pioneer in pursuing a strategy of vertical integration in the clothing industry with its distribution network. This strategy has allowed the company to collect and exploit information about sales and consumers to enhance its responses to the market.

According to Hansted, Blomqvist and Posner (2004, p. 36):

> H&M's decision to keep CSR messages out of its marketing communications is clearly strategic. The reason is that their CSR efforts do not constitute a point of differentiation that makes shoppers choose H&M over other brands. Shoppers choose H&M because the company offers fashion and quality at a reasonable price. Thus as price is a key part of its value proposition, H&M does not want to be seen as an excessive philanthropist with profits to share for charities and not for consumers.

Body Shop

Body Shop International PLC, which was established in 1976 by Anita Roddick, is a leading global retailer of high-quality skin and body-care products. The firm has approximately 2,000 stores in 54 countries, including Europe, the USA, the Middle East, Africa, and the Asia–Pacific region. As a producer and marketer of ethically sourced and naturally based beauty products, Body Shop is regarded as one of the pioneers of the modern CSR movement. For example, in 1996 Body Shop was one of the first companies to publish a 'values report'. Body Shop was sold to L'Oreal in 2006.

Body Shop's brand identity has been its 'profits-with-a-principle' philosophy, which has associated the brand with a social-justice agenda. Since its inception, the company has championed various social issues that complement its core values – such as opposition to animal testing, the development of 'community trade', campaigning for human rights, and protection of the environment.

Body Shop's innovative concept was to develop cosmetics without using animal testing. The company also has a focus on ethical consumption and social issues. Its commitment to these corporate values has provided the brand's essential identity (Kent and Stone, 2007).

Body Shop is a member of the UN Global Compact and its service culture is based on TBL thinking. It promotes a culture for sustainable business through community development and involvement of its stakeholders. As a values-based company, Body Shop communicates its core values through its relationships with its stakeholders – including employees (who are referred to as 'our people').

According to Kent and Stone (2007, p. 538):

> L'Oreal itself claimed to promote similar principles to Body Shop ... and sought to take advantage of its ethical marketing skills, specifically in community trade. The acquisition also enabled L'Oreal to build its portfolio of smaller brands, a trend more generally evident in many major US corporations that have developed an interest in purchasing smaller, values-oriented companies ... There has been a shift from pragmatic, price and value driven imperatives towards 'real values' – the bundle of meanings that suggest a brand is adopting a definable position in an understood moral or ethical framework. In the corporate perception at least, The Body Shop remains a standard bearer of 'real value' in the 2000s.

Comparison of IKEA, Starbucks, H&M, and Body Shop

A new entrepreneurial business model

All four companies were founded by energetic entrepreneurs: Kamprad at IKEA; Schultz at Starbucks; Persson at H&M, and Roddick at Body Shop. All of these entrepreneurs have been innovative in their various consumer industries. They have built distinctive business models in their companies, and these have been retained and developed over decades through the dissemination of the entrepreneur's values throughout their organisations.

All four companies also have a business model for future success based on: (i) various forms of TBL thinking; (ii) attractive offerings in attractive stores; and (iii) strong supplier chains governed by social and environmental responsibility and the requirements of good citizenship. In addition, they have growth strategies based on investment in sustainable resources – IKEA in energy conservation and managing social and environmental responsibility; Starbucks in recycling and community development; H&M in environmentally friendly products; and Body Shop in sustainable products. All four companies have strong corporate values and a clear focus on serving customers in a broad international target market.

The logic of values and the logic of value creation

In accordance with the logic of value creation, all four companies exert control over the design and development of the service offering and use suppliers in the value chain to control price, time, and quality. Moreover, in all four companies, the logic of value creation is driven by the logic of values. All take a TBL perspective with respect to logistics, stores, and production, and all have their own codes of conduct to ensure that their social, environmental, and quality standards are maintained. They also attempt to engage their suppliers in positive empowering relationships that create value for the suppliers themselves.

Service experience

All four companies have a focus on serving customers and have developed management policies and systems with regard to the co-creation of value with customers. The IKEA policy promotes customer placement in store showrooms ('experience rooms'). For Starbucks, customer-oriented policy is described as promotion of the 'Starbucks experience'. H&M promotes shopping as an easy and pleasant experience. Body Shop aims for an enjoyable customer experience in their shops and at home. In all four cases, customer-oriented policies aim to promote favourable service experiences.

Service brand and marketing communication

All four companies have well-known values-based global service brands. However, they do not explicitly use CSR in their market communication. All of these brands are positioned in accordance with the firm's views on environmental and social responsibility. The firms ensure that their brands are supported by the communities with whom they do business, that their suppliers are empowered, and that they engage with a range of environmental and social initiatives.

Service leadership

In all four companies, the knowledge and 'drive' of employees are of fundamental importance in developing a strong corporate culture with regard to 'living the brand' and sharing corporate values. Within IKEA, employees are referred to as 'co-workers'; Starbucks refers to 'partners'; H&M uses the term 'colleagues' and Body Shop talks about 'our people'.

All service leaders are expected to act as role models. Leadership performance is judged in terms of operational skills, cooperation with others, and sharing values and meanings. All four companies focus on investing in leadership performance and focus on the development of individual leaders and employees as a key strategy for company success. All the firms also seek leaders from diverse backgrounds to create a multicultural employment environment. Gender equality in employment is a goal of all the companies.

Five principles for a sustainable values-based service business

From the comparative analysis presented above, five principles for a sustainable values-based service business can be derived.

Principle 1: Strong values drive customer value

Strong values form the basis for a company culture. In tandem with customers' values and the values of the wider society, strong corporate values provide energy and direction to business development. Innovative service businesses are often created by entrepreneurs who are imbued with a clear vision and a strong sense of mission. Such a vision and mission are usually based on a firm set of personal values.

A company with strong values does not necessarily have unchanging values. Rather, values are dynamic and can become stronger in the sense that they become clearer, more relevant, and better integrated in the business model. Such values are used by customers and other stakeholders when value is assessed. The values create bonds with customers and thus represent a significant loyalty driver.

In summary, in developing a sustainable values-based company, values are pre-eminently important in the company's relationships with its staff, partners, suppliers, shareholders, and the media.

Principle 2: CSR as a strategy for sustainable service business

Sustainable values-based service businesses have a strong commitment to corporate social responsibility (CSR), which leads to quality-assurance systems, appropriate performance indicators, TBL thinking, and involvement with NGOs in assessments and improvement efforts.

A sense of social and environmental responsibility stimulates lean production, lean consumption, energy conservation, and the creative use of apparent 'waste'. Social and environmental responsibility thus contributes to profitability in a long-term perspective.

CSR is important for rethinking the role of any company in any industry. By using CSR in a proactive way, companies think 'laterally' in searching for 'smart' solutions. The logic of values thus drives the logic of value creation.

Principle 3: Values-based service experience for co-creating value

Many services are experience-based and companies should therefore create and offer 'test-drives' of services for customers to enable them to experience the service before purchase and consumption.

Customers' experiences are formed during consumption of a service. When a customer's basic requirements are met, other issues make a difference. These issues are often subtle, affective, and values-based. A well-designed service concept should include an 'experience room' to stimulate the service for customers.

Principle 4: Values-based service brand and communication for values resonance

Brands are living expressions of what a company stands for. They communicate what its products or services can do for people. However, if a company overstates what its products can do, and subsequently fails to deliver (as perceived by customers), this creates adverse reactions – both in the market and among the company's employees.

Successful brands are not created *de novo*; rather, they develop naturally within values-based companies. These brands then enable values-based companies to reach out and connect with customers, staff, and other stakeholders.

Successful companies often challenge established views in suggesting something new and attractive in their marketing. These ideas can be provocative, but they must simultaneously resonate with the values of customers in the market. Values-based brands must incorporate values that are attractive to customers and avoid being associated with unfavourable values. Values resonance (both within the organisation and outside it) is essential for a sustainable values-based service company.

Using CSR to secure a values-based service brand is more than mere communication about CSR with the customers; rather, it is about using CSR as basis for strategy and ensuring that the service brand (and communication with all stakeholders) is in resonance with the company's values, the customers' values, and the values of the wider society.

Principle 5: Values-based service leadership for living the values

To secure sustainability, a values-based company needs strong leadership. A company built on an entrepreneurial business model often has the original entrepreneur's values and leadership style as a model for future generations of leaders. However, the challenge for subsequent leaders is to develop these values and communicate what they mean today.

To communicate these values in contemporary terms, it is essential that leaders 'live' the values. Leadership is about 'walking the talk'. Both the 'talk' and the 'walk' must make sense to employees and energise them to focus on serving customers, thus creating shareholder value. Leaders communicate through their interactions with employees, partners, suppliers, and customers. Authentic leaders therefore spend time with customers and employees and learn from them. Great leaders are directed not only by the logic of value, but also by the logic of values.

A model for values-based service businesses

It will be recalled that Figure 1.1 in Chapter 1 presented a matrix of two value-creation logics (service-dominant logic and goods-dominant logic) on the vertical axis and two business models (a control-based business model and a values-based business model) on the horizontal axis. It will be apparent that the four innovative service companies discussed in this chapter all base their value creation on the *service-dominant logic* and that their business models are *values based*. All four companies are therefore firmly situated in the upper-right quadrant of Figure 1.1, as shown in Figure 7.1.

It is not suggested that these four companies are the only global businesses that would be situated in this quadrant. Many companies are now recognising the implications of sustainable development and the importance of values-based stances with respect to the environment and social responsibility. As Hart (2007, p. 3) has noted:

> Business – more than either government or civil society – is uniquely equipped at this point in history to lead us toward a sustainable world in the years ahead. I argue that corporations are the only entities in the world today with the technology, resources, capacity, and global reach required. Properly focused, the profit motive can accelerate (not

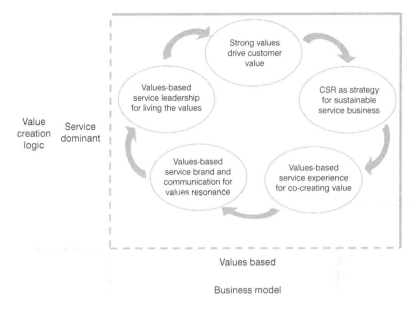

Figure 7.1 A model for values-based service for sustainable business

inhibit) the transformation toward global sustainability, with nonprofits, governments, and multilateral agencies all playing crucial roles as collaborators and watchdogs.

Gore (quoted in Hart, 2007, p. xxiv) has expressed a similar view:

The interests of shareholders, both public and private, over time, will be best served by companies that maximize their financial performance by strategically managing their economic, social, environmental, and ethical performance.

All of the companies discussed in this chapter have well-developed processes for renewal and reconfiguration of their business models in the light of experience over time (Normann, 2001). Renewal is essential for sustainable success.

The overriding orientation of all the companies described here is a genuine focus on the customer. Superior customer value is based on favourable service experiences, a strong brand, and dynamic marketing communication. This requires staying close to the customers, understanding their requirements, and providing solutions that are in accordance with their values and lifestyles. Learning from (and with) customers in various ways is crucially important if a company wishes to remain customer focused.

Corporate social and environmental responsibility has been demonstrated to be profitable – both in the short term and in the long term. Innovative service concepts that utilise physical products as platforms for service and customer experiences can create value-in-use. The logic of values and the logic of value are synergistic, profitable, and sustainable.

Questions

1   What do values mean in creating value for your customers and other stakeholders?
2   In what way does your business model include CSR?
3   How should a company interact with NGOs in pursuing CSR?
4   Compare your organisation with the five principles suggested in this chapter. What are the differences and similarities? What can your company learn?
5   What values have a significant impact on your service business?
6   How does the leadership 'live the values' in your company?
7   Do service experiences play a role in customer value in your company?
8   Describe how the service brand contributes to a sustainable service business in your company.
9   What roles do shared values and shared meanings play for values resonance in your company?

References

Hansted Blomqvist, K. and Posner, S. (2004) Three strategies for integrating CSR with brand marketing. Social Issues. *Market Leader* Summer, www.warc.com/MarketLeader.

Hart, S.L. (2007) *Capitalism at the Crossroads: Aligning Business, Earth, and Humanity*, 2nd edition. Upper Saddle River, NJ: Wharton School Publishing.

Kent, T. and Stone, D. (2007) The Body Shop and the role of design in retail branding, *International Journal of Retail & Distribution Management*, Vol. 35 No. 7, pp. 531–43.

Michelli, J.A. (2007) *The Starbucks Experience: 5 Principles for Turning Ordinary into Extraordinary*. New York: McGraw-Hill.

Normann, R. (2001) *Reframing Business: When the Map Changes the Landscape*. New York: John Wiley.

Vogel, D. (2005) *The Market for Virtue. The Potential and Limits of Corporate Social Responsibility*. Washington, DC: Brooking Institution Press.

Werther, W.B. and Chandler, D. (2005) Strategic corporate social responsibility as global brand insurance, *Business Horizons*, Vol. 48, pp. 317–24.

Appendix 1

A Furniture Dealer's Testament by Ingvar Kamprad

To create a better everyday life for the many people

By offering a wide range of well-designed, functional home furnishing products at prices so low that as many people as possible will be able to afford them.

We have decided once and for all to side with the many. What is good for our customers is also, in the long run, good for us. This is an objective that carries obligations.

All nations and societies in both the East and West spend a disproportionate amount of their resources on satisfying a minority of the population. In our line of business, for example, far too many of the fine designs and new ideas are reserved for a small circle of the affluent. That situation has influenced the formulation of our objectives.

After only a couple of decades, we have achieved good results. A well-known Swedish industrialist-politician has said that IKEA has meant more for the process of democratisation than many political measures put together. We believe, too, that our actions have inspired many of our colleagues to work along the same lines. Sweden, our "domestic market," has become a world pioneer in that many of the new concepts have been devised right from the outset for the benefit of the many – for all those with limited resources. We are in the forefront of that development.

But we have great ambitions. We know that we can be a beneficial influence on practically all markets. We know that in the future we will be able to make a valuable contribution to the process of democratisation outside our own homeland too. We know that larger production runs give us new advantages on our home ground, as well as more markets to spread our risks over. That is why it is our duty to expand.

The means we use for achieving our goals are characterised by our unprejudiced approach, by "doing it a different way" if you will, and by our aim to be simple and straightforward in ourselves and in our relations with others. Lifestyle is a strong word, but I do not hesitate to use it. Part of creating a better life for the many people also consists of breaking free from status and convention – becoming freer as human beings. We aim to make our name synonymous with that concept too – for our own benefit and for the inspiration of others. We must, however, always bear in mind that freedom implies responsibility, meaning that we must demand much of ourselves.

No method is more effective than the good example

I claimed earlier that we contribute to the process of democratisation. Let me add, to avoid any misunderstanding, that this does not mean that we take a position on questions of equality – such as salary issues. Though you may say that here again, we approach these problems from a different perspective.

Our product range and price philosophy, which are the essence of our work, are described in the following chapters. They also describe the rules and methods that we have worked out over the years as cornerstones of the framework of ideas that have made and will continue to make IKEA a unique company.

20 December 1976
Ingvar Kamprad

1. The product range – our identity

We shall offer a wide range of well-designed, functional home furnishing products at prices so low that as many people as possible will be able to afford them.

Range

The objective **must** be to encompass the total home environment, i.e. to offer furnishings and fittings for every part of the home whether indoors or outdoors. The range **may** also include tools, utensils and ornaments for the home as well as more or less advanced components for do-it-yourself furnishing and interior decoration. It **may** also contain a smaller number of articles for public buildings. The range must always be limited to avoid any adverse effect on the overall price picture. The main effort must always be concentrated on the essential products in each product area.

Profile

The main emphasis must always be on our basic range – on the part that is "typically IKEA". Our basic range must have its own profile. It must reflect our way of thinking by being as simple and straightforward as we are ourselves. It must be hard-wearing and easy to live with. It must reflect an easier, more natural and unconstrained way of life. It must express form, and be colourful and cheerful, with a youthful accent that appeals to the young at heart of all ages.

In Scandinavia, people should perceive our basic range as typically IKEA. Elsewhere, they should perceive it as typically Swedish.

Alongside the basic product range, we may have a smaller range in a more traditional style which appeals to most people and which may be combined with our basic range. This part of the range must be **strictly limited** outside Scandinavia.

Function and technical quality

"Throw-away" products are not IKEA. Whatever the consumer purchases shall give long-term enjoyment. That is why our products must be functional and well made. But quality must never be an end in itself: it must be adjusted to the consumer's needs. A tabletop, for example, needs a harder-wearing surface than a shelf in a bookcase. In the former case, a more expensive finish offers the consumer long-lasting utility, whereas in the latter it just hurts the customer by adding to the price. Quality must always be adapted to the consumer's interests in the long-term. Our benchmarks should be the basic Swedish Möbelfakta requirements or other sensible norms.

Low price with a meaning

The many people usually have limited financial resources. It is the many people whom we aim to serve. The first rule is to maintain an extremely low level of prices. But they must be low prices with a meaning. We must not compromise either functionality or technical quality.

No effort must be spared to ensure our prices are perceived to be low. There shall always be a substantial price difference compared to our competitors, and we shall always have the best value-for-money offers for every function. Every product area must include "breathtaking offers", and our range must never grow so large as to jeopardise our price picture. The concept of a low price with a meaning makes enormous demands on all our co-workers. That includes product developers, designers, buyers, office and warehouse staff, salespeople and all other cost bearers who are in a position to influence our purchase prices and **all our other costs** – in short, every single one of us! Without low costs, we can never accomplish our purpose.

Changes in our range policy

Our basic policy of serving the many people can never be changed. Changes in the guidelines given here concerning the composition of our product range can be made only by joint decision of the Boards of Ingka Holding B.V. and Inter IKEA Systems B.V.

2. The IKEA spirit – a strong and living reality

You have certainly experienced it. You may even have given it your own interpretation. Obviously it was easier to keep alive in the old days when there were not so many of us, when we were all within reach of each other and could talk to each other. It is naturally harder now that the individual has gradually been lost in the grey conformity of collective bargaining and the numbered files of the personnel department.

Things were more concrete in those days – the readiness to give each other a helping hand with everything; the art of managing on small means, of making the best with what we had; the cost-consciousness to the point of being stingy; the humbleness, the unconquerable enthusiasm and the wonderful sense of community through thick and thin. But both IKEA and society have changed since then.

But the spirit is still to be found in every one of our workplaces. Among old co-workers and new ones. Heroic efforts are still being done – daily – and there are many, many who still feel the same way. Not everybody in a large group like ours can feel the same sense of responsibility and enthusiasm. Some undoubtedly regard the job simply as a means of livelihood – a job like any other. Sometimes you and I must share the blame for failing to keep the flame alight, maybe for faltering in our own commitment at times, for simply not having the energy to infuse life and warmth into an apparently monotonous task.

The true IKEA spirit is still built on our enthusiasm, from our constant striving for renewal, from our cost-consciousness, from our readiness to take responsibility and help out, from our humbleness in approaching our task and from the simplicity of our way of doing things. We must look after each other and inspire each other. Those who cannot or will not join us are to be pitied.

A job must never be just a livelihood. If you are not enthusiastic about your job, a third of your life goes to waste, and a magazine in your desk drawer can never make up for that.

For those of you who bear any kind of leadership responsibility, it is crucially important to motivate and develop your co-workers. A team spirit is a fine thing, but it requires everybody in the team to be dedicated to their tasks. You, as the captain, make the decisions after consulting the team. There is no time for argument afterwards. Take a football team as your model!

Be thankful to those who are the pillars of our society! Those simple, quiet, taken-for-granted people who always are willing to lend a helping hand. They do their duty and shoulder their responsibility without being noticed. To them, a defined area of responsibility is a necessary but distasteful word. To them, the whole is just as self-evident as always helping and always sharing. I call them stalwarts simply because every system needs them. They are to be found everywhere – in our warehouses, in our offices, among our sales force... They are the very embodiment of the IKEA spirit.

Yes, the IKEA spirit still lives, but it too must be cultivated and developed to keep pace with the times. **Development is not always the same thing as progress.** It is often up to you, as the leader and bearer of responsibility, to make development progressive.

3. Profit gives us resources

A better everyday life for the many people! To achieve our aim, we must have resources – especially in the area of finance. We do not believe in waiting for ripe plums to fall into our mouths. We believe in hard, committed work that brings results.

Profit is a wonderful word! Let us start by stripping the word profit of its dramatic overtones. It is a word that politicians often use and abuse. Profit gives us resources. There are two ways to get resources: either through our own profit, or through subsidy. All state subsidies are paid for either out of the state's profit on operations of some kind, or from taxes of some kind that you and I have to pay. Let us be self-reliant in the matter of building up financial resources too.

The aim of our effort to build up financial resources is **to reach a good result in the long term**. You know what it takes to do that: we must offer the lowest prices, and we must combine them with good quality. If we charge too much, we will not be able to offer the lowest prices. If we charge too little, we will not be able to build up resources. A wonderful problem!

It forces us to develop products more economically, to purchase more efficiently and to be constantly stubborn in cost savings of all kinds. That is our secret. That is the foundation of our success.

4. Reaching good results with small means

That is an old IKEA idea that is more relevant than ever. Time after time we have proved that we can get good results with small means or very limited resources. Wasting resources is a mortal sin at IKEA. It is hardly an art to reach set targets if you do not have to count the cost. Any architect can design a desk that will cost 5,000 kronor. But only the most highly skilled can design a good, functional desk that will cost 100 kronor. **Expensive solutions to any kind of problem are usually the work of mediocrity**.

We have no respect for a solution until we know what it costs. An IKEA product without a price tag is always wrong! It is just as wrong as when a government does not tell the taxpayers what a "free" school lunch costs per portion.

Before you choose a solution, set it in relation to the cost. Only then can you fully determine its worth.

Waste of resources is one of the greatest diseases of mankind. Many modern buildings are more like monuments to human stupidity than rational answers to needs. But waste costs us even more in little everyday things: filing papers that you will never need again; spending time proving that you were right anyway; postponing a decision to the next meeting because you do not want to take the responsibility now; telephoning when you could just as easily write a note or send a fax. The list is endless.

Use your resources the IKEA way. Then you will reach good results with small means.

5. Simplicity is a virtue

There have to be rules to enable a lot of people to function together in a community or a company. But the more complicated the rules are, the harder they are to comply with. Complicated rules paralyse!

Historical baggage, fear and unwillingness to take responsibility are the breeding ground for bureaucracy. Indecisiveness generates more statistics, more studies, more committees, more bureaucracy. Bureaucracy complicates and paralyses!

Planning is often synonymous with bureaucracy. Planning is, of course, needed to lay out guidelines for your work and to enable a company to function in the long term. But do not forget that **exaggerated planning is the most common cause of corporate death**. Exaggerated planning constrains your freedom of action and leaves you less time to get things done. Complicated planning paralyses. So let simplicity and common sense guide your planning.

Simplicity is a fine tradition among us. Simple routines mean greater impact. Simplicity in our behaviour gives us strength. Simplicity and humbleness characterise us in our relations with each other, with our suppliers and with our customers. It is not just to cut costs that we avoid luxury hotels. We do not need fancy cars, posh titles, tailor-made uniforms or other status symbols. We rely on our own strength and our own will!

6. Doing it a different way

If we from the start had consulted experts about whether a little community like Älmhult could support a company like IKEA, they would have undoubtedly advised against it. Nevertheless, Älmhult is now home to one of the world's biggest facilities in the home furnishings business.

By always asking why we are doing this or that, we can find new paths. By refusing to accept a pattern simply because it is well established, we make progress. We dare to do it a different way! Not just in large matters, but in solving small everyday problems too.

It is no coincidence that our buyers go to a window factory for table legs and a shirt factory for cushions. It is quite simply the answer to the question **why**.

Our protest against convention is not protest for its own sake: it is a deliberate expression of our constant search for development and improvement.

Maintaining and developing the dynamic of our business is one of our most important tasks. That is why I hope, for example, that we will never have two identical stores. We know that the latest one is bound to have several things wrong with it, but will nevertheless, all in all, be the best yet. Dynamics and the desire to experiment must continually lead us forward. **"Why"** will remain an important key word.

7. Concentration – important to our success

The general who divides his resources will invariably be defeated. Even a multitalented athlete has problems.

For us too, it is a matter of concentration – focusing our resources. We can never do everything, everywhere, all at the same time.

Our range cannot be allowed to overflow. We can never satisfy all tastes anyway. We must concentrate on our own profile. We can never promote the whole of our range at once. We must concentrate. We cannot conquer every market at once. We must concentrate for maximum impact, often with small means.

While we are concentrating on important areas, we must "lista" ourselves on others. "Lista" is a common term in Småland; it means doing what you have to do with an absolute minimum of resources.

When we are building up a new market, we concentrate on marketing. Concentration means that at certain vital stages we are forced to neglect otherwise important aspects such as security systems. That is why we have to make extra special demands on the honesty and loyalty of every co-worker.

Concentration – the very word means strength. Use it in your daily work. It will give you results.

8. Taking responsibility – a privilege

There are people at all levels in every type of company and community who would rather make their own decisions than hide behind those made by others. People who dare to take responsibility. The fewer such responsibility-takers a company or a community has, the more bureaucratic it is. Constant meetings and group discussions are often the result of unwillingness or inability on the part of the person in charge to make decisions. Democracy or the obligations for consultation are sometimes cited as excuses.

Taking responsibility has nothing to do with education, financial position or rank. Responsibility-takers can be found in the warehouse, among the buyers, sales force and office staff – in short, everywhere. They are necessary in every system. They are essential for all progress. They are the ones who keep the wheels turning.

In our IKEA family we want to keep the focus on the individual and support each other. We all have our rights, but we also have our duties. Freedom with responsibility. Your initiative and mine are decisive. Our ability to take responsibility and make decisions.

Only while sleeping one makes no mistakes. Making mistakes is the privilege of the active – of those who can correct their mistakes and put them right.

Our objectives require us to constantly practise making decisions and taking responsibility, to constantly overcome our fear of making mistakes. **The fear of making mistakes is the root of bureaucracy and the enemy of development.** No decision can claim to be the only right one; it is the energy that is put into the decision that determines whether it is right. It must be allowed to make mistakes. It is always the mediocre people who are negative, who spend their time proving that they were not wrong. The strong person is always positive and looks forward.

It is always the positive people who win. They are always a joy to their colleagues and to themselves. But winning does not mean that someone else has to lose. The finest victories are those without losers. If somebody steals a model from us, we do not sue them, because a lawsuit is always negative. We solve the problem instead by developing a new and even better model.

Exercise your privilege – your right and your duty to make decisions and take responsibility.

9. Most things still remain to be done. A glorious future!

The feeling of having finished something is an effective sleeping pill. A person who retires feeling that he has done his bit will quickly wither away. A company which feels that it has reached its goal will quickly stagnate and lose its vitality.

Happiness is not reaching your goal. Happiness is being on the way. It is our wonderful fate to be just at the beginning. In all areas. We will move ahead only by constantly asking ourselves how what we are doing today can be done better tomorrow. The positive joy of discovery must be our inspiration in the future too. The word impossible has been and must remain deleted from our dictionary.

Experience is a word to be handled carefully.

Experience is a brake on all development. Many people cite experience as an excuse for not trying anything new. Still it can be wise to rely on experience at times. But if you do so, you should preferably rely on your own. That is usually more valuable than lengthy investigations.

Our ambition to develop ourselves as human beings and co-workers must remain high. Humbleness is the key word. Being humble means so much to us in our work and in our leisure. It is even decisive for us as human beings. It means not just consideration and respect for our fellow men and women, but also kindness and generosity. Will-power and strength without humbleness often lead to conflict. Together with humbleness, will-power and strength are your secret weapons for development as an individual and fellow human being.

Bear in mind that **time is your most important resource**. You can do so much in ten minutes. Ten minutes, once gone, are gone for good. You can never get them back.

Ten minutes are not just a sixth of your hourly pay. Ten minutes are a piece of yourself. Divide your life into ten-minute units and sacrifice as few of them as possible in meaningless activity.

Most of the job remains to be done. Let us continue to be a group of positive fanatics who stubbornly and persistently refuse to accept the impossible, the negative. What we want to do, we can do and will do together. A glorious future!

Appendix 2

List of visits, interviews and project-work in IKEA

Bo Enquist visit to IKEA Kungens Kurva, Stockholm, Sweden. Interviews with co-workers and customers, studying showrooms as experience rooms, February 2003

Interview with Kerri Molinaro, country manager IKEA Sweden, and Paul Ekelschot, ComIn Manager in Helsingborg, Sweden, December 2003 by Bo Enquist

Interview with Åsa Hjort, Store Manager in Kuala Lumpur, Malaysia, October 2003 by Bo Edvardsson

Interview with Terrence Nielsen, Store Manager in IKEA, Singapore, December 2003 by Bo Edvardsson

Meeting and discussion with Michael Hay, Global Communication IKEA, at International symposium QUIS 9, Karlstad University, June 2004 by Bo Edvardsson and Bo Enquist

Bo Edvardsson and Bo Enquist visit to IKEA Sweden, Älmhult, Sweden together with Michael Hay, IKEA, August 2004

Bo Edvardsson and Bo Enquist workshop with Michael Hay, IKEA Services AB, for a joint scientific article, at the 'Sockerbruket' (the 'Sugarmill') in Helsingborg, Sweden, March 2005

Meeting with Marianne Barner, Communications Manager, IKEA Group, Helsingborg, Sweden, March 2005 by Bo Enquist

Meeting and discussion with Thomas Bergmark, Manager Social and Environmental Affairs, IKEA Group in Helsingborg, Sweden by Bo Enquist and doctoral student Samuel Petros Sebhatu, May 2005

Interview with Tommy Kullberg, CEO of IKEA Japan, by Bo Enquist and doctoral student Samuel Petros Sebhatu, May 2005 in Stockholm

Bo Enquist visit to IKEA Schaumburg, IKEA USA. Interviews with co-workers and customers, October 2005

Bo Enquist visit to IKEA Bäckebol, Göteborg, Sweden with Samuel Petros Sebhatu, April 2006. Interviews with co-workers, studying diversity among co-workers

Interview with Lars Engman, Design Manager, IKEA Sweden, Älmhult, November 2006 by Bo Enquist

Interview with Marianne Barner Communications Manager, IKEA Group, Helsingborg, Sweden, by Bo Enquist, December 2006

Interview with Göran Nilsson, Managing Director IKEA Family Services AB, in Helsingborg, by Bo Enquist, December 2006

Bo Enquist visit to IKEA North America service center for meetings, interviews and observations, the IKEA Conshohocken store, Philadephia and IKEA Elizabeth store, New York, February 2007

Meeting with Arvid Grindheim, Head of Compliance, IKEA Group Social & Environmental Affairs by Bo Enquist at 'Oslo conference on good governance and social and environmental responsibility', Oslo, March 2007

Interview with Susanne Jensert, Store Manager, Karlstad, Sweden, December 2007 by Bo Edvardsson

Telephone interview with Jeanette Söderberg, Country Manager, IKEA Sweden, by Bo Edvardsson and Bo Enquist, February 2008

Field work and master student projects in IKEA (tutored by Bo Enquist)

Hagenaar, B. and Hart, A. (2003) 'From "Köttbullar" till "Bokhyllor": a study concerning the customer experience at IKEA Kungens Kurva'. Master thesis CTF, ISMr program, Karlstad University, Sweden.

Hagenaar, B. and Hart (2003) *'A comparison of the customer experience at IKEA Schaumburg and IKEA Kungens Kurva'*. Field work in IKEA Kungens Kurva, Sweden and IKEA Schaumburg, USA, interviews with co-workers and customers. *Project work* CTF, ISMr program, Karlstad University, Sweden.

Paul, V. and B. Yu (2003) 'Towards a long-run perspective driven by value-based service culture: a case study of IKEA in China'. Master thesis CTF, ISMr program, Karlstad University, Sweden.

Paul, V. and B. Yu (2003) 'IKEA China – Managing the gap between national culture and organizational culture'. Field work in IKEA Germany and France, interviews with co-workers and customers in IKEA Bejing. Project Work CTF, ISMr program, Karlstad University, Sweden.

Katalin Farkas and Emilie Frizot (2006) 'IKEA France and Germany: what makes their success so different?' Master thesis CTF, ISMr program, Karlstad University.

Katalin Farkas and Emilie Frizot (2006) 'IKEA France and Germany: IKEA's values-based service brand from a cultural perspective'. Field work in IKEA Germany and France, interviews with co-workers and customers. Project work, CTF, ISMr program, Karlstad University.

YiJun Zhang (2006) 'Values-based service brands lighten customers' eyes. A case study of IKEA Shanghai, China'. Master thesis CTF, ISMr program, Karlstad University.

YiJun Zhang (2006) 'Field Report IKEA Shanghai'. Field work in IKEA Shanghai, interviews with co-workers and customers. Project work, CTF, ISMr program, Karlstad University.

Yunfeng Zhang (2006) 'The utilization and effect of the interdependent relationship between service culture and service strategy in the customer's perspective'. Master thesis, CTF, ISMr program, Karlstad University.

Yunfeng Zhang (2006) 'Field study about IKEA Beijing in China'. Field work in IKEA Beijing, China, interviews with co-workers and customers. Project, work CTF, ISMr program, Karlstad University.

Johansson, S., Neste, N. and Österåker, U. (2006) 'IKEA Family as a service management control system'. Case study of the customer club IKEA Family in the master course Service Management Control, Karlstad University.

Johansson, S., Neste, N. and Österåker, U. (2006) 'Välkommen in i familjen – värdeskapande genom interaktion' (Welcome to the family – co-creating through interaction). Master thesis in business administration about IKEA Family, Karlstad University.

Arezina, Z. and Persson, S. (2006) 'Good citizenship "the IKEA Way"', Master thesis about ethnic diversity in IKEA Sweden, Karlstad University.

Braunberger, B. and Ya Zhang (2007) 'Using code of conduct to assure values-based quality'. Master thesis, CTF, ISMr program, Karlstad University.

Braunberger, B. and Ya Zhang (2007) 'The evolution and function of IKEA's code of conduct – IWAY in its supply chain management'. Project work CTF, ISMr program, Karlstad University.

Comparative study of CSR practice in IKEA, Starbucks, H&M and Body Shop

The comparative study of Starbucks, H&M and Body Shop was done in parallel with the IKEA study during 2006 and 2007 and resulted in two written papers:

Enquist, B., Edvardsson, B. and Petros Sebhatu, S. (2007) Corporate Social Responsibility for Charity or for Service Business? (QMOD 10, Helsingborg, June 2007)

Enquist, B., Edvardsson, B. and Petros Sebhatu, S. (2007) Corporate Social Responsibility as Strategy for Innovative Service Business – A Comparative Study of IKEA, Starbucks, H&M and Body Shop. CTF/ Karlstad University (Work in progress)

Index